Praise for *Reinvention*

"I've seen firsthand in my work with top executives that the art of personal reinvention is more critical now than ever, yet leaders are left struggling with how to develop this vital capability. Cragun and Sweetman provide precisely what organizations and leaders need—a simple model and process for making major change and renewal sustainable."

—Cassandra Frangos, vice president, Global Executive Talent, Cisco Systems

"Viewing leadership as a force multiplier in the Reinvention Formula pushes leaders to rethink what matters most in their work! Put simply, for anyone or any organization to reinvent demands exceptional leadership behind the wheel. The authors deliver a serious handbook for navigating the 21st century."

—Hal Gregersen, PhD, executive director, MIT Leadership Center

"As the head of an Asian asset management firm investing in companies all over ASEAN, this book sings to me. Worldwide disruption is something I deal with everyday, and great leaders understand disruption and even disrupt others. What an incredible handbook for the 21st-century leader to ensure you always stay at the head of the pack!"

—Shireen Muhiudeen, founder, Corston-Smith Asset Management Malaysia; Forbes List 50 Power Asian Businesswomen.

"*Reinvention* is a terrific book that gives readers a complete picture of all of the elements needed for quantum change to happen and to stick. I especially appreciate the author's clear demonstration of how leadership is a force multiplier to every other element in their reinvention formula—at both the personal and organizational level. This contribution alone distinguishes it from other books on change. Filled with both insight and application, this engaging book delivers useful models and examples that are extremely relevant for our times. Well done!"

—Stephen M. R. Covey, *New York Times* best-selling author of *The Speed of Trust* and coauthor of *Smart Trust*

"*Reinvention* provides a practical roadmap that helps build highly adaptive individuals and organizations positioned to thrive in today's turbulent environment. The authors masterfully integrate the latest research and thinking with their firsthand global consulting experience to create powerful new thought leadership in the areas of leadership and change. This is a must read for today's leaders."

—Linda A. Hill, professor of business administration, faculty chair, Harvard Business School

"Cragun and Sweetman have done an admirable job assembling key elements of strategic and leadership thinking into an extraordinarily innovative process and framework for making radical change happen successfully. Reading this book will push your leadership thinking and actions in exciting new directions."

—Robert Galford, author of *The Trusted Advisor, The Trusted Leader, Your Leadership Legacy,* and *Simple Sabotage*

"Reinvention: Accelerating Results in the Age of Disruption is the go-to leadership book of the decade. Cragun and Sweetman play the role not so much as sages, but as trusted guides by your side, providing powerful and practical strategies and tools for immediate business application at the individual and organizational levels."

—Ranjini Manian, founder and CEO, Global Adjustments India;
author of *Doing Business in India for Dummies*

"Reinvention is a must read for any founder or executive looking to build an organization that can thrive in the age of disruption. The authors challenge the reader to relook at their worldviews by citing contemporary examples of what makes today's organizations win or lose. The *Reinvention Roadmap* provides a highly actionable framework to apply design thinking to create sustainable change."

—Mohit Garg, cofounder and chief revenue officer, MindTickle, ranked among
the top 50 most-innovative companies globally by TiE50

"Reinvention: Accelerating Results in the Age of Disruption is a practical guide to the art of reinvention and accelerated change. It contains wisdom for each of us, offering vivid stories, frameworks, and tools with strong intellectual rigor. The authors challenge the reader to accept the necessity of reinvention in today's VUCA world. This is a worthy read for every leader."

—Patricia W. Longshore, vice president, Global Educator Network,
Duke Corporate Education

"In *Reinvention*, Kate and Shane give us a brand new platform and new way of thinking to confront challenge's of today's global economy. The result of their book is striking in its ability to help us make better sense of our VUCA world. And on those inevitable days when our forecasts and predictive tools fail us, Kate and Shane challenge us to continue working the problem with world-class strategies and tools."

—Denis Sullivan, VP Workforce and Leadership Development,
Verizon Wireless (retired)

"This book suggests that big changes are coming and provides heartfelt reasons on why to respond proactively before you're run over. I enjoyed the grounded storytelling and engaging metaphors. Best of all, I am now certain that the internal rate of change within myself and my organization must be faster than the external rate of change around us. There is no neutral place. It is a powerful wake-up call that it is time to change myself!"

—Sylvia Ann Hewlett, founding president, Center for Talent Innovation;
author of *Forget a Mentor, Find a Sponsor* and *Executive Presence*

"Disruption: Either it's happening to you, or you are causing it. In the book *Reinvention*, Cragun and Sweetman describe, from their own experience and through a set of winning stories, how organizational leaders can plot a safe path through the disrupted landscape of the modern organization. It's a compelling, practical read."

—Robert M. Burnside, chief learning officer, Ketchum Inc.

"With incredible acuity, *Reinvention* proves the value of preemptive change in the face of unceasing disruption. It provides well-founded analysis and depth on how—and why—proactivity, not reactivity, will be the defining feature of successful companys in today's landscape. The authors' timely work makes it easy, through practical solutions and fresh concepts, to demystify the culture of change. It is a must-read for anyone looking to keep their company ahead of the curve."

—**Spencer Harrison, PhD,** professor of business, Carroll School of
   Management, Boston College

"What a tremendously important piece of work—reframing the way we must understand ourselves, our passions, and our companies as we nosedive deeper into 21st-century models of leadership. *Reinvention* is the key. Ready, aim, and reinvent with this book by your bedside table."

—**Marcia Jaffe,** founder and president, Bali Institute for Global Renewal

"The authors demonstrate a clear understanding of disappearing market borders, international regulatory frameworks, transforming multinationals, and an entirely new array of global risks, opportunities, and disruptions. Cragun and Sweetman remind us that many of the assumptions that defined our economies and us at the turn of the Millennium no longer apply. We need *Reinvention*."

—**Redha Behbehani,** executive director, Global Center, the College of
   Business Administration, Kuwait University

"As change becomes the constant, adaptability is the number-one key to the future success of business. *Reinvention* teaches us all how to transform as leaders and companies to navigate the changing generational mindset to achieve breakthrough results and grow into the future. Anyone in a leadership position today or who aspires to be in one in the future should read this book."

—**Erica Dhawan,** author of *Get Big Things Done*; CEO of Cotential;
   former Legatum Scholar, MIT

"*Reinvention* is about profound change—the kind needed to cope with the disruptive forces that are changing the way we work and live. This book lays out the reasons for this disruption and provides a blueprint for navigating through to success in the 21st century. Sweetening this are remarkable insights from some of the best global thinkers about the future."

—**Kevin Wheeler,** president, Future of Talent Institute and
   Global Resource Center

"Cragun and Sweetman lay out powerful models and intuitive metaphors that you can actually see yourself implementing. The Six Blindfolds, followed up by the Reinvention Agility Matrix, seamlessly blend the theoretical and practical. This book is a must for individuals who want to shake things up in their career and for leaders ready to reinvent their organizations."

—**John Bingham,** MBA Director, Marriott School of Management,
   Brigham Young University

"*Reinvention* provides an incredible guide to all leaders today. This book should be required reading for all Asian entrepreneurs and business leaders. Asia is in the centre of exciting growth but also tremendous challenges. *Reinvention* will arm these leaders with the knowledge and platform to transform the typical Asian business into a future global company."

—**Gerard Teoh,** founder, Crave Capital, an Asian Advisory Company

"Using a variety of examples and stories, the authors make a strong case for the need to quickly and nimbly adapt—or face failure and extinction. The Reinvention Formula and the *Reinvention Roadmap* enable individuals and organizations to effectively respond to disruption through practical tools, models, and processes. This book is an important read for practitioners and students."

—**Judith Gordon,** chairperson, Management and Organization Department, Carroll School of Management, Boston College

"Having been engaged in hi-tech companies and Silicon Valley startups throughout my career, I was struck with how applicable the Reinvention Formula is to organizations of all shapes, sizes, and geography. Based on clear and universal principles, Cragun and Sweetman have written a timeless book that should be in the toolkits of 21st-century global professionals."

—**Mark Richards,** SVP Products, Jemstep; cofounder, NetMind and Sandhill Partners.

"*Reinvention* is an incredibly powerful resource guide for anyone or any organization to thrive—not just survive—in our rapidly changing world. The authors layout a Reinvention Formula that allows individuals and organizations to align processes, systems, and structures to achieve their new vision. A terrific book for proactive leaders excited about embracing the exciting changes that lie ahead!"

—**Chris Harrison,** president, Robson Communities

"This is a must-read for any leader looking to thrive in a world of constant change. Loaded with powerful frameworks, exercises, and stories, this book provides leaders with the tools they need to implement change in themselves and their organizations. Whether you're feeling the pressures of change or would simply like to stay ahead of the curve, look no look no further than this comprehensive and practical guide."

—**David M.R. Covey and Stephan Mardyks,** CEOs, SMCOV

"This book is impressive for its ability to describe in detail the brutal facts of doing business in today's global business environment and recommending powerful solutions to help the reader stay ahead of the curve. The authors should be applauded for sharing their practical advice and vast experience on this critical topic."

—**Amar Bhide, PhD,** professor, Fletcher School of Law and Diplomacy, Tufts University

REINVENTION

REINVENTION

Accelerating Results in the Age of Disruption

◇◇

SHANE CRAGUN
KATE SWEETMAN

GREENLEAF
BOOK GROUP PRESS

Published by Greenleaf Book Group Press
Austin, Texas
www.gbgpress.com

Distributed by Greenleaf Book Group

For ordering information or special discounts for bulk purchases, please contact Greenleaf Book Group at PO Box 91869, Austin, TX 78709, 512.891.6100.

Design and composition by Greenleaf Book Group and Sheila Parr
Cover design by Greenleaf Book Group and Sheila Parr
Cover image © iStockphoto.com / ThomasVogel

Cataloging-in-Publication data is available.

Print ISBN: 978-1-62634-286-6

eBook ISBN: 978-1-62634-287-3

Part of the Tree Neutral® program, which offsets the number of trees consumed in the production and printing of this book by taking proactive steps, such as planting trees in direct proportion to the number of trees used: www.treeneutral.com

Printed in the United States of America on acid-free paper

16 17 18 19 20 21   10 9 8 7 6 5 4 3 2 1

First Edition

We dedicate this book to . . .

Shane

To my mentors . . . for taking a bet on me as an intern at National Semiconductor and teaching me the core blocking and tackling of my trade. Little did I know that Richard Feller and Paul Gustavson were planning on unleashing a young MBA graduate throughout international locations to further a turnaround that, three years later, would be recognized as the "Turnaround Company of the Year" by the *San Francisco Examiner*. I will never forget dinner at the Cape Arundel Inn in Maine after an offsite with the executive team. Richard, thank you for your gracious contributions to this book and for coming to BYU to hire me in the first place. Paul, thank you for teaching me the basics and continuing to wow me every time I see you in action.

Kate

To my mentors . . . for directly impacting my ability to make a difference throughout the world with both my clients and my writing. My greatest mentors have been Dave Ulrich, Norm Smallwood, Linda Hill, and Nan Stone. Dave and Norm, without your generosity, guidance, and cosmic patience I would be half the person and professional I am today. I still find myself asking, when I am facing difficult client challenges, "What would Dave and Norm do?" Linda, you are my ever-stalwart partner whom I continue to stop by and visit to seek advice when we both happen to be in Boston at the same time. Nan, thank you for hiring me as an editor at *Harvard Business Review*, despite my lack of editorial experience. You enabled me to work with many of the world's great minds in business management, and this inspired me to higher action.

CONTENTS

FOREWORD

It turns out we are the ones who introduced Kate and Shane to each other professionally years ago. We think this gives us bragging rights now that we see them teaming up and creating compelling and exciting new thought leadership.

Here's how the introduction happened.

In 2006, the US Securities and Exchange Commission told Citigroup that they were forbidden to make additional acquisitions. The SEC told Chuck Prince, the Citigroup CEO at the time, that Citigroup had to implement one vital thing to get in the clear. And that was to strengthen the ethical foundation within the company, particularly among top leadership.

Our firm, The RBL Group, was invited by Citigroup to develop a series of global ethics workshops to be delivered to the top 1 percent. This was our biggest project ever, and we knew we needed top-caliber talent to facilitate these sessions. Two of the gifted people we selected were Kate Sweetman and Shane Cragun.

This is their first book together, and it is a good one.

Reinvention: Accelerating Results in the Age of Disruption is a finely tuned call to action for both individuals and organizations hoping to survive and thrive in the 21st century.

The authors introduce "The Law of the 21st-Century Business Jungle: Quickly Adapt or Perish!" We like that. As the business environment continues to spin faster and faster, only those individuals and organizations capable of pivoting and reinventing quickly, proactively, and effectively will be able to maintain leading status and a commanding presence.

We found their illustrations and cases enlightening. For example, the actual newspaper headline in 1981 from a prominent daily that proclaimed:

100,000 Datsuns Arrive on Docks in Los Angeles. Inventory Sold in 90 Days!

That was a rousing reminder of how drastically things have changed in just three short decades.

We liked the "Six Deadly Blindfolds" metaphor because it provides evidence that, although we live in a world of remarkable change, and many of us have gone through leadership and change management training, individuals and organizations still seem to fall back into time-tested ways of slipping into irrelevance and sometimes failure.

This book has come at the perfect time.

You will learn a must-have competency that is fast becoming table stakes if you want to participate in today's global economy. That competency is the ability to make quantum change happen proactively when the need arises. Why would any of us engage in reactive strategies with our professional careers and with the organizations we lead?

We found the book simple and straightforward. It covers a lot of ground and provides models, diagnostics, and tools in each chapter to help the reader move from concept to action. The theories and concepts are based upon sound principles in the areas of change, leadership, and high performance.

The authors know their stuff. Pay careful attention to the recipe that they present. We believe you will enjoy looking at change from the unique lens this volume puts forth.

We are thrilled to endorse this book. Best to you as you begin your Reinvention journey.

Dave and Norm
Fall 2015

David Ulrich
Cofounder, RBL Group
Professor of Business,
University of Michigan
Named #1 Management Thinker
Author of 30 business books

Norm Smallwood
Cofounder, RBL Group
Named Top 100 Voices in
Global Leadership
Published over 100 articles
Author of eight business books

⟡⟡⟡⟡⟡⟡⟡⟡⟡⟡⟡⟡⟡⟡⟡⟡⟡⟡⟡⟡⟡⟡⟡⟡⟡⟡⟡⟡⟡⟡⟡⟡

SHIFTING INTO A HIGHER GEAR

RAISING YOUR GAME—INDIVIDUALLY AND ORGANIZATIONALLY

*"If you live each day as if it was your last, someday you'll
most certainly be right. Stay hungry. Stay foolish."*

—*Steve Jobs*

Living in the Age of Uber

We were recently at a wedding dinner in Boston honoring the daughter of a close friend from India. The daughter married a boy in the United States, and we were a few of the fortunate guests invited.

As the dinner was winding down, the younger sister of the bride was ready to call it a night. She exclaimed, "I'm getting Uber! Who wants to go back to the hotel with me?" She then began placing the order on her iPhone.

Within seconds she exclaimed excitedly, "A Suburban we can all fit in will be here in ten minutes." A few minutes later she nudged someone sitting next to her and asked, "Hey, shall I get a black one?" After getting confirmation that the color black was definitely the coolest of all color choices, she modified her order. And within ten minutes she and others climbed into a shiny, new black Chevy Suburban. And that was that.

In this Age of Uber, there are now more Uber drivers (ten thousand) in New York City than yellow-cab drivers. New York City cab drivers are seeing a serious decrease in their business, and are in the process of asking the government to intervene and protect their livelihoods.

But it is not just Uber disrupting the livelihoods of taxi drivers. We live in an Age of Disruption. Virtually everything is being disrupted.

Moore's Law Applied to Change

We suggest that the only constant going forward is *change*. We're talking massive, disruptive, and tumultuous change. We are now in the bit economy. And it is beginning to look like radical change will be THE absolute going forward in the 21st century.

With just a quick glance through the news, it becomes apparent that disruption is everywhere.

MIT's Media Lab announced that it has created a 4-D television that allows viewers to reach through the screen and touch the objects they are viewing. This might seem more like a gimmick than a game changer. But check this out.

Google recently declared that they want to be *THE* operating system for your life. Google wants to be everywhere you are. They've produced mobile software for your wrist, and are now focused on creating mobile software for your car and your living room.

Having cut our teeth in Silicon Valley, we suggest that a version of Moore's Law will soon apply to the speed of change in the global business environment.

Gordon Moore was one of the original Intel cofounders. In 1965 he predicted that the number of transistors per square inch on integrated circuits (microchips) would double every year going forward. And he has been right. We suggest that the speed of change in the global business environment will eventually reach a point where it is doubling every year.

Why Reinvention Matters

This book was written to help you and your organization grow your ability to facilitate significant change when the need arises. And, we suggest, make that major pivot even before seismic change interrupts your world.

Based upon years of study and experience on the subject of individual and organizational high performance, we suggest that the ability to reinvent yourself and reinvent your organization will be one of the most important competencies to master in the 21st century. In fact, having the ability to reinvent may simply become the price of admission to play in today's global game of business.

Accelerating Results During Disruption

We suggest that it will not be good enough going forward to simply survive incoming global shockwaves. The best organizations and leaders will be those who actually accelerate results and leapfrog the competition in the midst of revolutionary change.

These market leaders will possess an uncanny ability to use the force of incoming, highly disruptive change to emerge with superior competitive positioning and increased competitive advantage. They will have accelerated results in areas such as financial outcomes, customer loyalty, employee engagement, internal efficiencies, and market share.

Eventually, accelerating results during major disruption will become a highly sought after capability among leaders and organizations globally.

Currently, very few organizations have the capability to do this. It has been acceptable to simply survive the tumultuous global whitewater environment. Gold medals are handed out to victorious survivors! But, in the future, the ability to just "survive" massive disruption will be table stakes.

Those that learn how to leverage disruption to their benefit—and accelerate important scorecard targets and results—will be the market champions of the 21st century, the Age of Disruption.

Four Decades of Change Acceleration

In the 1980s, after the significant global competition was first introduced into the United States by the Japanese Big Three automakers (Honda, Toyota, and Datsun), a new buzzword seemed to come into vogue: "change."

In the 1990s, the need for companies to change seemed to intensify and accelerate and the new buzzword seemed to be "reengineer." In fact, within four years of Michael Hammer's book *Reengineering the Corporation* being published, approximately seventy percent of all Fortune 500 companies admitted they had already been reengineering processes. And in the 2000s the need for change seemed to fast track even more, and the new buzzword became "transform."

We suggest that going forward the new catchphrase for change will be "reinvent," where absolutely everything is on the table, and all assumptions are challenged in an effort to tackle major disruption in quantum and accelerated ways.

The Leader-Caretaker Myth

It's not enough anymore just to keep up. Or to be what we call a Leader-Caretaker. As professionals, we must constantly position ourselves mentally, emotionally, physically, and socially to boldly lead the pack into the headwinds of change.

Look what happened to Microsoft after 12 years of leadership under CEO Steve Ballmer. Ballmer was the ultimate Leader-Caretaker. He played defense, and avoided offense. He led as if his role was simply to keep the company afloat after Bill left.

Ballmer fought hard to maintain the status quo. He always seemed surprised when the moat around his company began shrinking. He felt that sticking with what made Microsoft successful in the past—core hardware and software—was the recipe for success forever and ever. But the share price spoke otherwise. It dropped under his leadership from sixty dollars in January 2012 to thirty dollars by the time he departed in February 2014.

What will be Ballmer's biggest legacy? In 2007 his management team pleaded with him to begin investing in cloud computing. Ballmer ignored these recommendations and instead placed all his bets on the doomed Vista operating platform.

On the other hand, there are leaders called Leader-Accelerators. These are the exceptional leaders of the 21st century. Leader-Accelerators think big and make things happen under almost any circumstance. They blow life and energy into people and processes. They have an incredible multiplier effect on results.

Elon Musk qualifies as a Leader-Accelerator. He is the serial entrepreneur behind PayPal, Tesla, SpaceX, and Hyperloop. He was recently quoted as saying, "I would like to die on Mars. Just not on impact."

Does leadership thinking get any bigger than that? Caretaking is no longer an option in today's Age of Disruption!

REINVENTION DEFINED

We define Reinvention as

"Quantum Individual and Organizational Change Accelerated."

To be successful, you and your organization must have the ability to reinvent, pivot, and morph faster than the speed of the external environment that you operate within. Possessing the ability to not only survive disruption but also accelerate results during turbulent and challenging times is a skill that must be mastered.

What the Future Holds

It's getting harder for futurists to predict upcoming changes in the global business environment. These strategists can no longer depend upon past trends for predictions. After all, just a decade before the World Wide Web became commonplace in 1996, there was very little buzz about its potential, or even its existence.

Although we may not know for certain what future global disruptions might be, we can be certain that they are already locked and loaded in the pipeline and are being prepared to launch.

Silicon Valley entrepreneurs are now vowing to disrupt entire industries. Hearing this, a Fortune 500 CEO recently commented anonymously that he and his fellow chief executives are now more concerned about the competition coming from the Bay Area than from traditional sources of competition.

Disruption indeed.

And although many of the new ideas, technologies, and disruptions may emanate from Palo Alto and its neighboring cities, the phenomenon of disruption is clearly global.

Disruption Emanating from Nontraditional Geographies

We recently met Omar Christidis, the Lebanese founder and CEO of ArabNet.

ArabNet was launched in 2009 to help grow the web and mobile sectors in the Arab world. The intention was to stimulate growth in the digital knowledge economy throughout MENA (Middle East and North Africa). This would help create high-quality, knowledge-driven careers for young Arabs.

We were fortunate to attend the 2015 ArabNet conference in Dubai. The conference placed special emphasis on ways to disrupt traditional banks across MENA through peer-to-peer lending, crowdfunding, mobile payments, electronic payments, crypto-currencies, and more.

One speaker cited the acceleration of global investment in FinTech start-ups. FinTech companies are newly funded companies with the purpose of disrupting incumbent financial organizations. Fueled by venture capital and private equity, Anthony Butler, of *The Political Quarterly*, calls this investment infusion the "Cambrian Explosion of Start-ups."

What Happened to My Job?

To get our minds around the topic of quantum global change, let's take a look at what futurist Graeme Codrington predicts for three of the world's most prevalent jobs in the future:

- **Private bankers, wealth managers, and stock traders:** Dynamic programming and algorithmic engineering will eventually replace these positions. Most stock exchange floor traders are gone, and backroom traders are now struggling to keep their jobs. Stocks and commodities are being traded by complex and lightning-fast algorithmic platforms. As soon as these new machines have the capability to recommend the best ROI, private bankers and wealth managers will eventually disappear.

- **Frontline military personnel:** The military employs many young people who need jobs. But the US military is in the process of removing frontline military troops and replacing them with robots, drones, and other mechanical fighting machines. Advanced military forces like China and Russia will quickly follow. Eventually, people toggling video-like consoles in rooms far away from enemy fire will fight tomorrow's battles.

- **Lawyers and accountants:** Artificial intelligence machines will eventually replace these white-collar jobs. The main tasks of these professions are crunching and dispensing valuable advice to clients. But scientists are making great strides in creating computers that are capable of intelligent behavior and thought.

Codrington is quick to point out, however, that whenever an economy replaces old jobs, many new jobs spring up. For instance, although frontline troops in the military might be replaced, there will be a high demand for new military roles such as drone operators, robot designers, and cyber warfare experts.

But this raises a question: who will be prepared for these new jobs when they come online? We believe it will be those who proactively pursued cutting-edge education and skills training and who invested time and energy into making the necessary changes to their lives. These fortunate individuals will have anticipated job shifts ahead of others, and many will reinvent before they have to.

Changing Because You Choose to

Proactive personal change agents will be the winners in the new economy and in the growing on-demand marketplace.

The right approach to dealing with incoming change is to change *before* you have to versus change *because* you have to. Why not be proactive? Besides, who owns your career path and career trajectory other than you? And who is in charge of running your team, department, or organization at work?

Proactive strategies have always proven to be better than reactive strategies in terms of individual and organizational high performance. It's better to make change happen on your own terms and within your own time frame.

Universal Principles of Change

This is the first business book to propose a reinvention-change methodology that works effectively for both individuals and organizations.

While writing this book, we actually tried to disprove this point. We asked, "Should we write two different books because the principles of reinvention are different for individuals versus organizations?" But we kept coming back to a singular thought: the principles of making quantum change happen individually and organizationally are the same. It is about moving from a current, less desired state to a future, more desired state with the many complexities that entails.

Our Reinvention Formula's core backbone originates from the revolutionary work of David Beckhardt in 1969. It is truly remarkable that Beckhardt created this simple yet powerful model when the need for change in the US business environment was negligible. He was a pioneer and genius before his time.

He left us powerful models to build from many decades later. We are not sure Beckhardt could have predicted that an Age of Disruption would hit so hard and so fast in the future. We've refined and added to his model in ways that make it supremely relevant for today's era.

Our Background in Change

As authors, we have more than fifty years of combined experience working with clients in the areas of individual and organizational change, leadership, strategy, redesign, and high performance. Many of our projects have been global in nature and have occurred in virtually every industry and in every region of the world. We have labored as internal consultants, external consultants, and executives. We've seen the same picture from three different directions.

After a while, you begin to identify clear patterns of what works and what doesn't work when trying to make change happen and ultimately stick. It becomes obvious which theories written in business books are effective, and which theories should have remained just theories. Despite differences in cultures around the globe, there seems to be a common set of principles around reinventive change that transcend borders and continents.

New Concepts Presented in Our Book

We hope we have written a practical book that can be used as a resource guide in navigating change on a daily basis. There are several concepts we're eager to introduce:

The Age of Disruption: We live in the Age of Disruption, where the status quo is being challenged like never before and continues to accelerate in speed and complexity.

- **The Global Shockwave 20:** The twenty core global events that have driven the warp-speed business environment we operate in today.

- **The 21st-Century Competitiveness Cycle:** Two Age of Disruption Principles that are predictive of an organization's current and future competitiveness.

- **The Law of the 21st-Century Business Jungle:** A powerful law, like gravity, that is firmly in place and must be acknowledged when leading yourself and your organization if you hope for success to occur.

- **The Six Deadly Blindfolds:** Six fundamental reasons individuals and organizations tend to slip into irrelevance and ultimately fail.

- **Reinvention Agility Matrix:** The judo-oriented metaphor that describes the four different ways individuals and organizations respond to disruptive change.

- **The Message of Mavericks:** Proposing two principles called "To Buoy or Not to Buoy" and "To Disrupt or Be Disrupted" that predict a person's or organization's ability to identify, and prepare for, incoming global shockwaves.

- **Reinvention Formula and Reinvention Roadmap:** A simple algorithm used to facilitate successful reinventive change that accelerates results. And a comprehensive roadmap, game plan, and template that provide eleven specific activities to make reinvention a reality.

- **Leadership as the Force Multiplier:** Leadership is at a premium, and nothing force multiplies results, for better or worse, than leadership at the individual, team, organizational, or societal levels.

- **Reinvention Evaluations:** Valuable benchmarks that convey where you and your organization stand in relation to the need and readiness for reinvention.

- **Reinvention Accelerators:** Five enabling strategies that accelerate successful reinvention: 1) Adopting Effective Leader Sets; 2) Leveraging Whole-Brain Thinking; 3) Crafting a Powerful Leadership Brand; 4) Being a Reinvention Champion; and 5) Preserving Work–Life Balance

- **Accelerating Results during Disruption:** Market leaders in the future will leverage global shockwaves to accelerate results versus simply trying to survive the whitewater.

Defining True Success

We recently spoke to 350 entrepreneurs representing 40 different countries at a conference in Dubrovnik, Croatia. It was powerful to mingle with foreign colleagues and to understand the desires and challenges they faced. Every participant seemed to have a burning desire to make a difference in the various industries and nations they represented.

The speakers were excellent. But there was one speaker from the United Kingdom, a personal wealth coach, who created a hush among the audience when he espoused a principle that rang true to all listening.

He said, "Your passion, not your career, is what defines you. Nobody cares what you do. They care who you are."

As we dash around trying to maintain profitability despite massive change, this powerful idea of focusing on "who you are" versus "what you do" seems critical. It is essential that we hold tight to those fundamental core values and characteristics that make us effective at leading others and leading ourselves.

Perhaps the noblest gift we can give colleagues is our time, attention, and compassion when they struggle professionally or personally under the burden of today's disruptive environment.

Practicing What We Preach

We've partnered with our publisher to innovate the layout and format of this book. Why not practice what we preach and do a little disrupting of our own?

Instead of typical chapter summaries, we have asked six global leadership, change, and innovation experts from different industries, knowledge domains, and geographical business regions to provide their unique insights and learnings for each chapter. We appreciate the investment each of them has made to make this truly a global book.

Taking the Reinvention Challenge

If you choose to take the challenge of reinvention, we invite you to share with us your experience. We are creating a community of reinventors and would enjoy having you on our team.

We facilitate four global think tanks—Global-Virtual Thought Leadership Clouds—that are comprised of thought leaders from different knowledge domains and regions throughout the world. Each Cloud publishes on a semiannual basis the best global knowledge and best practices in the four intangible areas that focus on Leader-Acceleration, Shared Energy, Vibrant Innovation, and Change Mastery. Reinvention is a component within the Change Mastery Cloud.

Please visit www.ageofdisruption.com to become part of our community.

Shane Cragun and Kate Sweetman
Boston, Massachusetts, 2016
www.ageofdisruption.com

◇◇◇◇◇◇◇◇◇◇◇◇◇◇◇◇◇◇◇◇◇◇◇◇◇◇◇◇◇◇◇◇◇◇◇◇◇◇

Chapter One

THE AGE OF DISRUPTION

SEISMIC CHANGE, ENORMOUS SHIFTS,
AND SWEEPING UPHEAVALS: WELCOME TO
TODAY'S BUSINESS ENVIRONMENT!

"Failure isn't fatal. But failure to change might be."

—*John Wooden*

Food Fights and Icebergs

Perhaps you've heard recently how the trillion-dollar US food industry is at a critical tipping point. More and more shoppers are opting for fresh, organic choices, and this is costing packaged food companies serious market share. In fact, the top twenty-five US food and beverage companies have lost more than $18 billion in value since 2009. And that trend is picking up steam.

An Edward Jones analyst suggested that the major food labels' fundamental existence is being challenged. The big questions in the food industry are these: can industry leaders reinvent fast enough to right the ship? And can they transition from being organizations that are decelerating to ones that are back on track?

Much of this depends on the eventual outcome of a powerful metaphor we discovered while researching this subject. A respected industry analyst offered this: "I would think of these big food companies like melting icebergs. Every year they become a little less relevant."

Wow. Melting icebergs.

With that, let's begin by asking four "Confront the Brutal Facts" questions to get the conversation started.

1. **Melt-Rate:** Is your professional or organizational iceberg melting? If so, at what rate? And why?

2. **Relevance Trend:** Are you and the organization you lead increasing in relevance in the eyes of customers and shareholders or decreasing in relevance? Why, or why not?

3. **Adding Value:** Do you continually push yourself and your organization to add greater value to customers and stakeholders? Why, or why not?

4. **Internal vs. External Change:** Is your current and projected rate of internal change greater than the current and projected speed of external change? Why, or why not?

How would you answer these questions for yourself and for the organization that you lead?

The Age of Disruption

We've coined the term Age of Disruption to describe the global business environment we currently work in. The term seems apt, because most of the changes that come our way are disruptive in nature. They disorient and disrupt the hard-earned flow state that many of us have settled into individually and organizationally.

We've all experienced that awkward feeling when colleagues begin chatting about a new technology that they love but we've never heard of. Suddenly, you get a queasy feeling that you are falling behind in an ever-changing world.

Add to that the fact that the total amount of information created in 2015 surpassed the zettabyte mark—a 1 with twenty-one 0s after it—and the prospect of staying current and relevant individually and organizationally begins to feel overwhelming.

Technology writer Michael S. Malone notes: "The higher level of anarchy we are living in will be exciting, but it will also be painful. Entire industries will die overnight, laying off thousands, while others will just as suddenly appear, hungry for employees. Continuity and predictability will be the rarest of commodities."

Recent research suggests that graduates leaving college today can expect to have at least sixteen different career changes during their work life.

Era of the Free Agent

Some talent futurists are predicting that nearly thirty-three percent of today's employees will eventually be working "on demand." This refers to the increasing preference of companies to hire freelancers for short-term contracts when the need arises, versus keeping full-time staff on the payroll.

It seems the W-2 is making room for the rise of the 1099.

We like how Susan Ascher, a professional recruiter from New Jersey, boils it down to a simple thought when talking about the age of the 1099: "The long-standing social contract between companies and workers has been officially broken. A permanent job is now a temporary job disguised with benefits."

How Did We Get Here?

Our research suggests it was in 1981 that the world became aware that the global economy was beginning to transition to something never experienced before.

In 1981 Toyota, Honda, and Datsun (the Japanese Big Three) sold more cars in the United States than analysts had predicted; it was also the first year they sold their cars from their own dealerships. This was a game-changing event on a global scale that had never been seen before by global leaders and professionals.

Industry observers intuitively knew that something monumental was happening. But even then, no one predicted this global shockwave would soon be followed up by many others. Global competition had literally washed up on the shores of the US West Coast and had taken everyone by storm.

Detroit responded in disappointing ways. They continued to cling to their worldview that Japanese products were inferior, faulty, and of no threat. Detroit leaders could not fathom the idea that their economic moat could be penetrated by the Japanese. And this was despite front-page newspaper headlines that proclaimed such things as

100,000 Datsuns Arrive on Docks in Los Angeles. Inventory Sold in 90 Days!

In hindsight, it is clear that the introduction of global competition in the form of Japanese automobiles was the "shot fired across the bow" of the US business sector. It was also a loud signal to the global business environment that change was coming. The days of US businesses running on autopilot without robust competition, yet still making healthy profits, were on their way out.

The Global Shockwave 20

We began our historical research on the Age of Disruption by searching for and uncovering key events in the past that seemed to have a profound effect on today's business ecosystem.

We started our research in the post-war decade (1946) and marched forward to 2015. In total, we identified twenty powerful global events that occurred during these seven decades that seemed to truly rattle the birdcage. We named these events Global Shockwaves because of their powerful ability to shock and disrupt the status quo.

A shockwave is defined as "a widespread feeling of shock caused by an unexpected event."

When you view these global shockwaves from a strategic level, and analyze the sequence of their arrival, a clear and compelling picture develops as to why we operate today in such turbulent times.

The following timeline depicts the global shockwaves in order of occurrence. We also note the year that the global shockwave's ripple effect had the biggest effect on the psyche of global organizations and the leaders that led them. In some cases, the year noted is not when the actual shockwave was initially felt.

We have categorized these global shockwaves into five types.

- **Technology:** Information and computing technologies.
- **Management theory:** New ways to think about managing people, manufacturing products, and creating greater revenues, lower costs, and increased speed.
- **Economic:** Wall Street–influenced fears, central banking actions, market fluctuations, and global supply and demand.
- **Global competition:** Exporting or importing goods on a global scale.
- **Geo-Political:** Tensions between nations caused by geographic, economic, religious, or political disputes.

THE GLOBAL SHOCKWAVE 20

Age of Disruption Global Shockwave Timeline

Biggest Effect	Global Shockwave	Category
1981	Rise of Global Competition	Global Competition
1989	Introduction of User-Friendly Hardware/Software	Technology
1991	Fall of Soviet Union	Geo-Political
1991	Thought Leaders Challenge Status Quo	Management Theory
1993	Creation of European Union	Geo-Political
1995	Reengineering of Business Processes	Management Theory
1995	Interconnected Global Telecommunications	Technology
1995	PCs Become Ubiquitous	Technology
1996	Commercialization of World Wide Web	Technology
1997	Advent of E-Commerce	Technology

(Continued)

Biggest Effect	Global Shockwave	Category
1999	Downsizing and Layoffs	Economic
2001	Intensification of Terrorism	Geo-Political
2004	Implementation of Outsourcing and Offshoring	Management Theory
2006	Mainstreaming of Smartphones	Technology
2007	Dawn of Social Media	Technology
2008	Onset of Global Recession	Economic
2010	Standardization of Virtual Workforce	Management Theory
2011	Introduction of Arab Spring	Geo-Political
2012	Escalation of Cloud Computing	Technology
2015	Collapse of Crude Oil Prices	Economic

It is interesting to note that forty percent of all global shockwaves are technology oriented. Going forward, the prediction is that the percentage of technology shockwaves will continue to climb in number.

Four of the global shockwaves were in the Management Theory category, and four were in Geo-Politics. Clearly, management thought leaders have had a crucial impact on how global business operates today, and geo-political challenges always shake things up.

Although only three global shockwaves were economic in nature, the second one—the Onset of the Global Economic Recession—continues to send tremors throughout all regions of the world and is continuing to have a devastating economic impact in Europe and parts of Asia.

Appreciating the twenty global shockwaves is helpful, but understanding the patterns behind each will better help business leaders more effectively predict new, incoming shockwaves and face them with greater confidence and certainty.

The Perfect Storm

In some cases, shockwaves can actually combine to create even larger disruptions than are typical. They can create "A Perfect Storm" situation in which entire industries and global regions are impacted.

In 1991, the Andrea Gail, a commercial fishing vessel out of Gloucester, Massachusetts, sank in the North Atlantic with her six-person crew. The crew had been fishing in the violent Grand Banks fishing grounds.

The last radio transmission from Captain Billy Tyne was "She's comin' on, boys, and she's comin' on strong." At the time of his transmission, Captain Tyne and his crew were right in the most ferocious part of the storm.

The cause of that fateful 1991 storm was the convergence of three powerful weather events at the same time. Although rare, and only occurring once every seventy-five years, when it does happen it creates what weather researchers call "the perfect storm."

In the Andrea Gail's case, two powerful opposing weather fronts created a monster northeaster. It then combined shortly thereafter with Hurricane Grace. This record storm produced wind gusts of up to 93 miles per hour and waves as high as sixty feet. It was a towering wave that eventually took the Andrea Gail under.

The Power of Cause and Effect

The flowchart below depicts an example of a Perfect Storm that happened in the global business environment in the mid-to-late 1990s. Several of the twenty shockwaves interacted to cause challenging situations.

THE GLOBAL SHOCKWAVE 20
Key Cause-and-Effect Relationships (1995–1998)

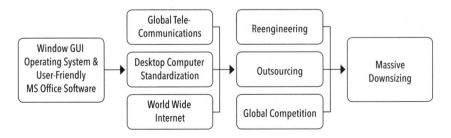

Notice the cause-and-effect impact throughout the chain. To create the massive global layoff environment of the past two decades (the box on the far right), three powerful shockwaves occurred at virtually the same time: Reengineering, Outsourcing and Offshoring, and Global Competition. In 2004 alone, 3,170,000 people were laid off just in the United States.

The 21st-Century Competitiveness Cycle

We began this chapter asking four questions in order to start the conversation on the issue of not only surviving, but accelerating in the Age of Disruption. Let's do a deeper dive on the fourth question: "is our rate of internal change currently greater than the rate of external change?"

In the Age of Disruption, the ability to survive, thrive, and accelerate results—both individually and organizationally—is directly tied to your ability to outpace the change in your external environment.

The 21st-Century Competitiveness Cycle—or the ability to compete in the Age of Disruption—is based upon two Age of Disruption Principles that we encourage our clients to tightly align with and create metrics around. They are always in play no matter the market, industry, or geography.

AGE OF DISRUPTION	
Principle 1: *Today*	**Principle 2:** *Tomorrow*
"To win today, individuals and organizations must be able to change internally faster and more dynamically than the speed and magnitude of external change."	"To win tomorrow, individuals and organizations must create internal change capacity and capability faster than the rate of change projected to happen externally."

Azim Premji, known as the Czar of the Indian IT revolution, was onto this notion when he wrote, "When the rate of change outside is more than what it is inside, be sure that the end is near." Mr. Premji is actually hinting at a harder-hitting truth: Extinction is inevitable when the above Age of Disruption Principles are violated.

Incoming Global Shockwaves Ahead

It's unlikely we will experience a cluster of five massive disruptive shockwaves like those that combined during the 1995–1998 time period. Each of these shockwaves by themselves had a powerful influence on today's global business environment. But together, they created a sonic boom that continues to be felt today.

Most futurists predict significant change over the next two decades, mostly from new technologies. But these same futurists agree that they foresee nothing in the shockwave pipeline as significant as the introduction of the personal computer, global telecommunications, and the Internet.

But you never know. And that is the lesson.

While we can't yet predict when or how the next global shockwave will manifest itself, one thing is certain: shockwaves will hit. And you and your organization do not want to be left isolated in the breakdown lane on the global highway watching the competition pass you by at superior speeds because they out-prepared you.

How prepared will you be when the 21st shockwave arrives at your doorstep?

Expert Insight: Murali Krishnamurthy

Our era is rightly called the Age of Disruption by the authors because the set of large forces defined in this book have dynamically interacted over the past 35 years to shift the very energy of our planet away from stability to turbulence. It will be a long time before those forces are spent. The future belongs to the people who are energized by the possibilities and to individuals, organizations, and societies that develop the capacity to capitalize on them.

The good news is that these individuals, organizations, and societies can deal with sudden and disruptive change—even get ahead of it—when they are alert to what is happening and when they have a roadmap for action coupled with the desire and discipline to act on it. The past 35 years have shown much success as well as failure.

Key Insights

The most important insights for me in this chapter were the following:

Global Shockwave 20
Consider for a moment that I am someone who left his native India before its economic liberalization as a young man in search of opportunity, and I am also someone who worked in the United States as an engineer during a technology boom and bust—and lost his engineering job in the process. I have both ridden and been pulled under by these shockwaves and fully understand their awesome power to both create and destroy.

Food Fights and Icebergs
Irrelevance can happen faster than it can be imagined. Even the largest and most powerful industries can be threatened by unexpected sources: from overseas, from a parallel industry, or from customers themselves.

21st-Century Competitiveness Cycle: Age of Disruption Principles 1 and 2
The demands on leadership will be greater and greater as the organization deals with change not as an objective to be met but as a vector quantity that must be managed dynamically virtually forever: an uncontainable energy with magnitude and direction but no real end.

Incoming Shockwaves
My former leader at Intel, Andy Grove, said famously, "Only the paranoid survive." People who spend their time up the mast, peering from the crow's nest, looking for trouble on the horizon, as well as opportunity, will eventually find both. The more keenly they look, the better chance they have of dealing with both well.

Era of the Free Agent
The explosion of entrepreneurship in India is a direct result of economic reforms. Many young Indians are grabbing this historic opportunity and running with it.

Application to My Career

It is impossible to read about these shockwaves and not see India being both battered and uplifted by them.

Battered when the Soviet Union fell, the ripple effect on the socialist Indian economy almost bankrupted the nation. It was uplifted when technology and globalization created unprecedented opportunities for outsourcing.

In 1991, as the economy slowed from even its sluggish "Hindu rate of return" of two to three percent to zero, the budget could no longer function under the multiple burdens of state control, government subsidies, tariffs and trade barriers, crippling red tape, and corruption. Only the actions of Prime Minister P. V. Narasimha Rao and his team saved us by reinventing the Indian economy overnight from socialism to a much more free economy. They unleashed the energies that ultimately became India Inc.

India has also exported a large number of workers to many other countries, where they have thrived by reinventing themselves. Many have taken full advantage of the opportunities made possible by the shockwaves, have educated themselves, worked very hard, and excelled in technology, medicine, and many other fields.

Advice to the Reader

As an individual, you need to be prepared to do what it takes to thrive in the Age of Disruption. Doing so is often difficult. For Indians to thrive in the shockwaves facing our nation, they often had to make the very difficult choice to reinvent themselves in a new land. Indians traditionally live in very supportive networks of extended families. Any Indian who ventured abroad likely made a choice that was very unpopular and countercultural to his or her family.

Simply seeing the global shockwave is not enough. As an individual or as an organization, you must plan and prepare yourself to be strong enough and skilled enough to ride it. In my case, I pursued my bachelors and my masters in engineering in a foreign land. Are you willing to do what it takes to be prepared to thrive?

About the Expert

Murali Krishnamurthy is the Founder and Executive Chaiman of Sankara Eye Foundation, which raises funds for free eye surgeries in India (see www .giftofvision.org).In his role, Krishnamurthy recruited, motivated, and challenged volunteers to bring out their potential to achieve more. The results: SEF expanded from 8,000 free eye surgeries in 1998 to more than 106,000 free eye surgeries in 2010.

Krishnamurthy is a graduate of NIT Trichy and the University of Illinois–Carbondale.

Chapter Two

<><><><><><><><><><><><><><><><><><><><><><><><><><>

THE SIX DEADLY BLINDFOLDS

WHY INDIVIDUALS AND ORGANIZATIONS SLIP INTO IRRELEVANCE AND ULTIMATELY FAIL

"Some people don't like change, but you need to embrace change if the alternative is disaster."

—*Elon Musk*

Race to the South Pole

In 1911 the race was on between the British and Norwegians to be the first nation to reach the South Pole. Englishman Robert Scott led the British team, and Norwegian explorer Roald Amundsen led the Norwegian team. During what is known as the Heroic Age of Antarctic Exploration, great honors and riches went to the victors.

Both leaders had strong teams, plentiful resources, and access to the same information. They even ran the race at the same time in the same season. They had the same technologies to choose from.

But one team far outperformed the other.

The Norwegian team beat the British team to the South Pole by thirty-four days. And, tragically, Scott and his British comrades perished on their way back to their original supply depot. All six bodies were found in the spring.

What was the difference between the performances of both teams? They had the same starting point, the same conditions, the same opportunities and challenges, and an open abundance of resources and new technologies.

The distinction was in the leaders themselves.

The Difference between Life and Death

Those who later studied the race concluded that the difference in Amundsen's and Scott's attitudes and worldviews was at the root cause behind the difference in performance.

Scott was stubbornly British and felt it was Britain's destiny to be the first to the South Pole. He played it safe and simply stuck with what had worked best in the past. In fact, he prided himself on his stubborn resolve and unwillingness to bow to change despite the extremes of the Antarctic.

Amundsen, on the other hand, was keenly aware that there were always new and better ways to do things. He had a practical outlook, which could be summed up with a question he would often ask: what will work best in order to win the prize? Amundsen gathered information whenever and wherever he could and was willing to try new processes to succeed.

Arrogance versus Humility

Scott was a die-hard British Navy man who proudly adhered to every tradition that implied. He and his officers kept a proper British distance from the enlisted men, going so far as to section them off during meals with a sheet strung across the tent. Amundsen, on the other hand, made sure mealtime was an opportunity for all to be together and share stories and learnings.

Another contrast between the two leaders was how much each was willing to learn from others, quickly develop skills and expertise, and then do things in better ways. Amundsen and his crew had the curiosity and humility to learn from two winters spent with the Netsilik Inuit people in northern Canada.

As a group, the Norwegians learned how to work with sled dogs for transportation, and, should the situation warrant it, as a food source. They learned that animal skins were warmer than wool and kept the wearer dry even when they were wet on the outside.

As a result of his research, Amundsen made the strategic decision to use one-hundred Greenland dogs, the best and strongest available, to provide the muscle behind the movement and to eventually provide his men with furs when the dogs were spent. When they broke down, the dogs could also provide food for other dogs and food for his men.

Ponies or Dogs

With little knowledge of, or even curiosity about, the Antarctic, Scott made the fateful decision to draw his sleds with ponies for half of the trip, and then use his men as the beasts of burden for the last half.

A quick look at a pony, with its small hooves relative to its large body, reveals that it is ill-suited to work effectively on snow and ice without snowshoes. But ponies had been established as Britain's best beasts of burden, and Scott stuck with the status quo.

Børge Ousland, a Norwegian explorer who made the first solo crossing of the Antarctic years later, gave his perspective on Amundsen: "I am inspired by how Amundsen prepared his expeditions. He always tried to learn from others. He identified the problem and then looked for a solution."

Amundsen later recorded that he did not understand the apparent aversion the British explorers had to dogs. He scribbled, "Can it be that the dog has not understood its master? Or is it the master who has not understood the dog?"

Contemporary Examples of Irrelevance and Failure

To understand how to effectively reinvent both individually and organizationally, we found it helpful to begin researching why individuals and organizations slip into irrelevance and sometimes fail.

We examined contemporary organizations that were going in the wrong direction. Five of those organizations are found in the table below with a few story lines about their situations.

As you browse through each example, try to identify the primary theme that stands out as the core reason for their poor performance or even extinction.

Company	Status	Story Line
RadioShack	On Life Support	RadioShack used to cater to hobbyists who liked to build their own computers, used CB radios, and needed specialized parts to repair home electronics. RadioShack sold one of the first mass-produced personal computers in the 1980s called the TRS-80. But the chain lost whatever early-mover advantage it had in the PC market and took computers off the shelf. RadioShack instead focused on becoming the place to buy batteries and electronics parts, and a place to get your electronics repaired. Neither strategy has worked, and the future does not look promising.
Swissair	RIP	The former national airline of Switzerland, Swissair, used to be so financially stable that it was known as the "flying bank." Founded in 1931, Switzerland's national icon eventually shut their doors in 2002 after years of being supported by the government. Unlike other global airlines, Swissair was never able to rebound from the hit airlines took after 9/11. Swissair also refused to join the important airline alliances, such as Star Alliance.
BlackBerry	Off the Ventilator	BlackBerry's launch of the first smartphone in the mid-2000s was sensational. It wasn't called a Crackberry for nothing. BlackBerry phones were the most popular mobile devices on the market. That is, until iPhones and Droids suddenly appeared. These revolutionary touch-screen smartphones turned the BlackBerry into an antiquated device. But despite this, BlackBerry thought their unique and patented QWERTY keyboards would still attract professional and business-oriented people. So they confidently continued to build products without a touch screen. And that was the wrong bet. People switched to the iPhone and the Android in droves because of their overall features and performance.
Blockbuster Video	DOA	Blockbuster was once an incredibly successful video rental chain that survived the transition from VHS to DVD just fine. But Blockbuster leadership then failed to adapt to the next big industry change: Netflix and the Internet. The death knell for Blockbuster came when streaming video became available through online outlets. Blockbuster had not prepared for that. And to their very last day, Blockbuster kept clutching tightly to their business model of retail store outlets.

Company	Status	Story Line
Sony	On a Slippery Slope	Japanese electronic giants once ruled the global electronics landscape. But not anymore. Sony, for example, is losing its competitive advantage and becoming just a me-too company. Gaming is increasingly moving to the phone and tablet, but Sony has continued to focus on the gaming device. In addition, in the past ten years they have implemented only incremental innovations at meeting customers' changing needs rather than disrupting the marketplace with new ideas.

What do these five examples have in common when it comes to slipping into irrelevance or going extinct? It is their inability to quickly adapt to a fast-changing external business environment.

So let's lock in a critical principle we must adhere to in today's Age of Disruption if we want to achieve and sustain success. This truth led us to establish what we feel is a critical law that both individuals and organizations must understand and comply with in the 21st century if they want to have even a remote chance of success:

The Law of the 21st-Century Business Jungle: Quickly Adapt, or Perish!

Like the law of gravity, you can disagree with the Law of the 21st-Century Business Jungle, but it will remain a factor deeply rooted and in place despite your opinion and judgment.

Say Goodbye to the Steady State

We suggest that there is no such thing as a "steady state" anymore in today's business environment. Even those leading well-established and seemingly bulletproof companies and careers must continually adapt to a fast-shifting business environment.

A vivid example of this can be seen through the eyes of Ron Woodward. Woodward was the president of Boeing's Commercial Airplane Group a few decades ago.

The year was 1987, and Boeing had a virtual monopoly on the airliner industry. This was the first year Airbus showed the world that they had finally gained global scale. They won four hundred orders for their A320 flagship plane. In the past, these orders no doubt would have gone to Boeing.

Airbus had been formed back in 1970 as a European conglomerate focused on making and selling commercial airliners. Over the years they made no bones about their desire to compete head-to-head with Boeing. They were very open about their product development plans and new technologies they were testing.

Ron Woodward was interviewed a few years later and asked about the new global competition he was facing in the commercial airlines business. In the interview, Woodward admitted, "I remember the first time another company (Airbus) got an airline order. I was just stunned."

We were stunned that he was stunned! Arrogance and invincibility seemed to have pervaded the culture of Boeing over the years to the point they were blind to Airbus's threat.

Warning: Vision Loss Ahead

We suggest that the inability or unwillingness of leaders and organizations to identify external changes in the business environment, and then humbly yet bravely adapt to them, is caused by a form of "vision loss."

With regard to the human eye, vision loss is the decreased ability to see; things become distorted. And total blindness is the inability to see at all.

History shows that leadership and organizational vision loss or blindness is the "root cause reason" behind the number-one reason organizations fail: a failure to quickly adapt to a fast-changing business environment.

The Six Deadly Blindfolds

Below are six metaphorical blindfolds we believe leaders and organizations wear that cause varying degrees of blindness. We picked the term Blindfold because we are confident that these six deadly blindfolds are, in reality, self-imposed!

The blindfold examples we provide below are organizational in nature, but can easily be translated to a professional's career.

Blindfold 6 Avoiding the Unavoidable		Blindfold 1 Arrogance
Blindfold 5 Believing Problems Don't Exist	THE SIX DEADLY BLINDFOLDS	Blindfold 2 Negative Feedback Not Acknowledged Here
Blindfold 4 We Know What's Best for the Customer		Blindfold 3 Dismissing Competitors' Successes

Blindfold 1: Arrogance

Brazil Walmart

Walmart's international expansion efforts have never met the growth expectations of analysts. One case in point is Brazil Walmart. Launched in 1995, this strategic move was supposed to prove that parent company Walmart could establish strong roots in any country in the world and succeed.

But the Brazil Walmart experiment has been a series of stumbling fits and starts. Most agree that it is corporate arrogance as the root cause. The thinking among executives was that what worked in the United States would also work in the global economy. Wouldn't foreign consumers sweep into stores once doors opened?

Imposing a series of systems, processes, structures, and culture that worked in the US and expecting it to work elsewhere around the globe is a strong example of corporate arrogance. Walmart would do better in Brazil and other global locations like Germany and Korea by becoming more adept at learning about the peoples and cultures and treating the international community as equals.

Blindfold 2: Negative Feedback Not Acknowledged Here

NASA (National Aeronautical Space Agency)

NASA's Kennedy Space Center has been one of our favorite clients. During one of our projects in 2003, the Space Shuttle *Columbia* disaster happened. It was an emotional time.

The president of the United States assigned a team called the *Columbia* Accident Investigation Board (CAIB) to conduct a full study on exactly what caused the shuttle disaster. The common feeling was that it was the foam that broke off and struck the wing. On one of our visits, our client contact showed us the CAIB report findings. He read us the most telling finding of all: "We are convinced that the management practices overseeing the space shuttle program were as much a cause of the accident as the foam that struck the left wing. NASA should continue to remove communication barriers and foster an inclusive environment where open communication is the norm and a culture of trust and openness permeates all facets of the organization. The NASA organizational culture has as much to do with this accident as the foam."

The revelation was stunning. It wasn't the foam that struck the wing that initially set the disaster in motion. The potential for disaster was already in play because of NASA's culture of inability and unwillingness to address potentially negative feedback that bubbled up from below. There were many engineers who had actually predicted the foam break might happen.

Blindfold 3: Dismissing Competitors' Successes

Microsoft

Microsoft continues to refuse to give Apple credit for their great success this past decade.

We had a chance to visit Microsoft headquarters recently in Redmond, Washington, and meet with a key executive over strategy and market research. We were anxious to find out before our visit ended how Microsoft perceived Steve Jobs and Apple's incredible success. Our Microsoft executive obliged. And we were shocked at what we heard.

In a period of five minutes, this executive expressed three times that Apple's success was simply a matter of "luck."

He explained that Steve Jobs was initially going to open his risky retail outlets with only one product to sell: the computer. He then explained that Apple stores would have certainly failed, except that the iPod luckily came along at just the right time. We were stunned. Apple's success was based on luck? In a period of ten years, Steve Jobs helped to create seven new industries, not to mention his launch of successful retail stores. It was hardly a matter of luck.

Blindfold 4: We Know What's Best for the Customer

European Private Rental Property Industry

What do companies such as Housetraps, 9flats, and Wimdu have in common? All were founded in hopes of joining the new private rental gold rush started by Airbnb in 2008. And all three of these companies are becoming increasingly irrelevant. Close analysis shows that each have been unable to scale their business because they have never moved past the me-too strategies they were founded upon. These copycats had the "build it, and they will come" mentality.

In hindsight, they were reluctant to gather consumer research, differentiate themselves, and message that differentiation to the consumers. Their worldview, simply put, was this: "Airbnb is crushing it. We need to join this trend, and we know that customers will buy anything as long as we get our technology up and running. We know what's best for the customer."

Blindfold 5: Believing Problems Don't Exist

General Motors

General Motors is a recent example of a large company that wasn't willing to confront the brutal facts when critical problems were happening. In a way, they refused to "know what they already knew" and act decisively upon that knowledge.

Between 1990 and 2000, GM engineers and middle managers knew that ignition switches in their small cars were defective, leading to car crashes and even deaths. For a decade, they heard about customer complaints, read about crashes in the hometown newspapers, and fought lawsuits to combat the onslaught. Estimates suggest that there were several hundred crashes and an estimated forty-two deaths over the period, and GM was aware of them.

But GM never made an attempt to fix the ignition switch problem. And they refused to acknowledge, internally or externally, that a problem existed. It took congressional and legal action to get GM to acknowledge their massive negligence.

Reports suggest that the ignition switch issues were known among the teams within GM close to the situation. In fact, reports show that in many team meetings individuals would volunteer the challenging information as something to address, but leaders would end meetings with no action items or accountability assigned.

Blindfold 6: Avoiding the Unavoidable

The Greek Depression

Unemployment levels in Greece are at catastrophic levels, holding steady at twenty-five percent. In 2012, Greece's government had the largest sovereign debt default in history. On June 30, 2015, Greece became the first developed country to fail to make an IMF loan repayment. At that time, Greece's government had debts of €323 billion.

The Greek depression officially began in 2009. But government and business leaders refused to address the writing on the wall that had been festering for years. In a way, they were avoiding the unavoidable.

What was the writing on the wall that was so clear to see, and that would lead most people to believe that huge problems were ahead and the economic system unsustainable?

- **Lavish Pension System:** In 2012, Greece spent 17.5 percent of its economic output on pension payments, the most in the European Union.

- **Early Retirement and Benefits:** Because of misaligned benefits and government programs, the average Greek worker retires at age sixty-one, and some government workers retire as early as age forty.

- **Work Culture Issues:** The Greek worker psyche is often to pass the buck to remain unaccountable, with a worldview often of "if I don't get paid, then I can't pay you."

- **Tax Evasion:** The country has always struggled to collect taxes from its citizens, especially the wealthy.

Removing Self-Imposed Blindfolds

The antidote to organizational blindness is what we call Reinvention Agility.

Reinventive Agile people and organizations embrace change as an ongoing fact and a cost of doing business. They approach new industries, new technologies, new restrictions, and other disruptions with a glass-half-full mind-set. They look for opportunities to take their game to the next level when shockwaves come at them.

Reinventive Agile people and organizations don't wait to let market disruptions shape them. They instead proactively address and adapt to the new disruptions in a way in which they can influence and leverage the outcome.

The Judo Metaphor

In our consulting business, we use the analogy of judo when talking about how to handle incoming global shockwaves.

Judo is the only martial art form that is defensive in its attack. The premise of judo is to use the force of the attacker to your advantage. Thus, it relies heavily on throwing techniques, which are called *nage-waza*. Judo originated in 1880, when its founder, Jigorō Kanō, was motivated to stop bullying at local schools among students. He knew jujitsu, but wanted something more effective where a smaller force could defeat a larger force. Central to Kanō's vision for judo was the principle of *seiryoku zen'yo*, translated as "maximum efficiency, minimum effort." He stressed many principles of his new martial art, but nothing as powerful as this: "Resisting a more powerful opponent will result in your defeat, whilst adjusting to and evading your opponent's attack will cause him to lose his balance, his power will be reduced, and you will defeat him. This makes it possible for weaker opponents to beat significantly stronger ones."

When we train our clients to be change agents, we suggest they address incoming global shockwaves as judokas, or judo practitioners, would. The idea is to leverage the force of the incoming, disruptive change in a way that actually strengthens them and their company's position as a result.

THE PRINCIPLE OF ACCELERATING RESULTS

Reinvention Judo Champions leverage incoming global shockwaves to their benefit. Their willingness and ability to proactively confront major disruption enables them to not only survive but also to thrive and accelerate results. This leads to competitive advantages and widened economic moats that are intangible in nature and difficult for competitors to copy.

THE CASE OF HENRY, ELON, AND THE AUTO INDUSTRY

Although the Big Three (GM, Ford, and Chrysler) were incredibly aware of the major shockwave emanating from Japan in 1981, it is alarming when one understands how little change and reinvention Detroit has engaged in since. We ask with great curiosity: what else needs to happen in order for Dissatisfaction with the Status Quo to finally take hold? Where were the revolutionary leaders who could have reinvented that industry? What has caused such visual impairment?

Analysts were publicly calling out GM in the early 1990s for generating negative ad campaigns to dismiss the need for electric cars. GM leaders actually spent money to keep the status quo in place. In fact, it was at this time when GM put more focus on introducing the gas-guzzling Hummer than it put on anything else.

On the other hand, two Leader-Accelerators within the automobile industry that we can point to are Henry Ford and Elon Musk. Not only are these two Judo Champions, but they welcomed disruption and decided to create disruption as well.

Henry Ford revolutionized the auto industry by creating the first mass-produced vehicle that middle-income Americans could afford. He promoted employee well-being by paying assembly line workers $5 an hour. This was triple the amount of any other automaker. Ford wanted his workers to be able to buy a Model T. He introduced five-day workweeks and the eight-hour work shift. With the help of the assembly line technology, Ford introduced the first Model T in 1908, and the company was producing one million Model Ts a year by 1920.

Elon Musk co-founded Tesla in 2003. The South African–born entrepreneur has helped make Tesla the leading and most successful electric vehicle company in the world. Musk refused to follow the traditional protocol of the Big Three when producing cars. Not only does Tesla not make cars like other auto manufacturers, he also refuses to sell the same way. Musk follows the

(Continued)

system that Ford used in the Model T days and uses franchises to sell cars.

In Musk's spare time, he founded SpaceX, meant to disrupt space travel, and Hyperloop, which aims to send passengers between California's two major cities in forty-five minutes.

Henry Ford and Elon Musk: Leader-Accelerators and Judo Champions, indeed.

Reinvention Agility Matrix

The *Reinvention Agility Matrix* measures the willingness and capability of individuals and organizations to seek out, humbly accept, diligently explore, and quickly adapt to incoming shockwaves within their industry and marketplace.

Willingness simply refers to the general attitude and degree to which change is embraced. *Ability* refers to the skill-set and tool-set strength of those confronting the need for quantum change.

The Reinvention Agility Matrix suggests there are four general responses, and types of people, that manifest themselves when global shockwaves roll in. Notice the general percentages of people that fall into each of these four camps.

When incoming shockwaves approach you or your organization, which category do you traditionally fall into? And will that be enough going forward in the 21st century?

The Message of Mavericks

There are only two weeks a year when the surf at Mavericks is large enough to attract big-wave surfers from around the world. Although these big waves near Half Moon Bay, California, form during the winter months, they are hard to predict.

Mavericks was a tightly held secret until twenty years ago, when *Surfer* magazine discovered that a few tight-lipped locals were surfing there.

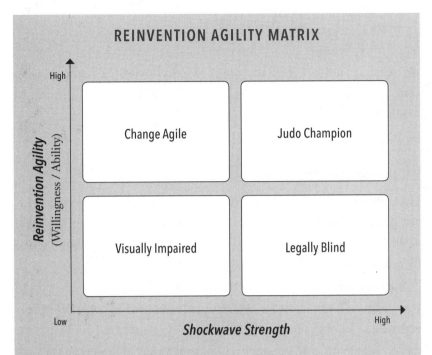

REINVENTION AGILITY MATRIX

High

Reinvention Agility
(Willingness / Ability)

Change Agile

Judo Champion

Visually Impaired

Legally Blind

Low

Shockwave Strength

High

Four Quadrants Defined

- **Judo Champion** (15 percent): They are the champions of change. They pride themselves on being the first ones on the block to adopt new innovations. They are focused on making quantum improvements and are thrilled by the idea of "change before you have to."

- **Change Agile** (45 percent): They have strong willingness and abilities in the Reinvention Agility Matrix, but prefer to take a wait-and-see approach. It is important for these people to understand the total benefit and ROI of the new change before they commit.

- **Visually Impaired** (35 percent): These people want solid evidence that the new changes proposed are must-haves. They are not fond of change and are comfortable sticking with the status quo or just incremental improvement. They can be vocal in their opposition to new ideas and approaches. But, given an ultimatum from man-agement, they will become good soldiers and grin and bear it.

- **Legally Blind** (5 percent): These leaders and employees will not change. They may nod their heads in agreement in a meeting, but they never change their underlying attitudes and hope they can wait out the new changes. They will often try to create a coalition of others who feel the same way they do. In many cases, they use guerrilla warfare techniques of fighting in the shadows.

In peak season, waves at Mavericks can average between twenty-five and eighty feet. These waves are known as the thickest waves in the world. They are dark in color compared with the brilliant aqua blue you see in other locations. This makes Mavericks deadly if you crash and burn.

When Do the Big Waves Break?

How do the world's best big-wave surfers, all of whom live in different places around the globe, know when the big swells are breaking at Mavericks? They listen each night to weather and wave forecasts broadcast from special radios they always carry.

These forecasts originate from specially placed buoys out in the Pacific Ocean. The buoys send information to meteorologists regarding the size of the swells approaching the coast of Northern California. When the swells reach a specific size, meteorologists send a Mavericks Alert message to the big-wave surfing community.

When this happens, it is not uncommon for surfers from around the world to be in their wet suits, on their long boards, and paddling toward a Mavericks swell one mile offshore within 48 hours. Surfer magazines also listen to the forecasts and send helicopters filled with people to photograph the event.

If we dive deeper into Mavericks as a metaphor, two messages and principles seem to leap out at us.

THE MESSAGE OF MAVERICKS

Mavericks Principle 1: To Buoy or Not to Buoy

Do you or your organization have "buoys" in place so that you are rarely surprised when powerful shockwaves begin pounding on your shore?

Great organizations and highly adaptive professionals seem to be better at predicting and understanding incoming changes than others.

Mavericks Principle 2: To Disrupt or Be Disrupted

We suggest that the change *before* you have to strategy is much better than the change *because* you have to approach. Why not introduce disruption and gain a first-mover advantage rather than maintaining a victim status?

Mavericks Principle 1: To Buoy or Not to Buoy

Do you or your organization have "buoys" in place so that you are rarely surprised when powerful shockwaves begin pounding on your shore?

Great organizations and highly adaptive professionals seem to be better at predicting and understanding incoming changes than others.

They are voracious readers and have a sense of the inevitable approaching. By the time the shockwaves manifest themselves at full impact, these Judo Champions are self-educated regarding the implications of the approaching shockwave and have a sense of what strategies they might employ for leveraging it.

Examples of individual buoys might be professionals asking their supervisor for additional performance reviews to assess their career trajectory, so they can be certain there are no surprising messages coming during year-end reviews. Another individual buoy might be subscribing to industry trade journals to search for clues about the future.

Examples of organizational buoys might be forming teams of leaders and employees to conduct environmental scans. This ensures better awareness of customer needs, competitor movements, and industry trends. Another organizational buoy might be conducting benchmarking exercises on firms outside your industry that are best-in-class in a competency you want to gain, so that you can leapfrog the competition in new and exciting ways.

Mavericks Principle 2: To Disrupt or Be Disrupted

We suggest that the change *before* you have to strategy is much better than the change *because* you have to approach. Why not introduce disruption and gain a first-mover advantage rather than maintaining a victim status?

Having well-placed buoys in your business environment will allow you to be much more proactive in taking control of and shaping your own destiny, whether that is being a disrupter or simply being prepared to leverage incoming shockwaves to your advantage.

Mai Boliang gets this. He is the CEO of CIMC, one of the world's largest container businesses. He and his Chinese company are Judo Champions on the Reinvention Agility Matrix.

They embrace change and practice the agility it takes to operate in today's Age of Disruption. Boliang is proud that he and his company constantly reinvent themselves in order to remain industry leaders. In his high-energy way, Boliang regularly tells anyone within earshot about his company's most important motto: "We learn, we improve, and we disrupt."

In an interview with an industry magazine, Boliang noted that much of CIMC's success has to do with its ability to predict and promptly react to business megatrends.

Employees like being led by Boliang. They feel safe in knowing that unfortunate surprises will likely not happen, and this frees them up emotionally to focus on their critical work.

Beautifully Equipped to Live in a World that No Longer Exists

There is no question that having a mind-set of "let's disrupt rather than be disrupted" makes someone feel more in control of their future.

A favorite quote of ours is from Eric Hoffer, a moral and social philosopher. Note that we have inserted the term *reinventor* to highlight the key lessons from this chapter.

> "In a time of drastic change, it is the learners [reinventors] who will inherit the future. The learned usually find themselves beautifully equipped to live in a world that no longer exists."

The race to the South Pole proves that the Age of Disruption rewards those who hold tightly to two key human traits: 1) humility, and 2) an eagerness to learn new things. We might add one more: the ability to believe in yourself and continue moving forward despite challenging times.

Martin Luther King Jr. relayed this thought perfectly when he said,

If you can't fly, then run. If you can't run, then walk. If you can't walk, then crawl. But whatever you do, keep moving forward!

Expert Insight: Constantinos Loizides

It seems that whole industries and markets are becoming obsolete—or are already obsolete—like print encyclopedia publishers and map makers, phone books, camera film, fixed telephone lines, fax machines, travel agencies, video arcades, public phone booths, and traditional television channels.

Something I know from my profession is that, eventually, cash itself will become obsolete.

Key Insights

There were several key insights for me from this chapter.

The Six Deadly Blindfolds

The six deadly blindfolds prevent individuals and companies from recognizing that times are quickly changing and that change is needed. As the digital age accelerates, globalization crushes barriers, and regulation increases costs, it is imperative for all companies to clearly see the risks of obsolescence. To have on top of that any of the six deadly blindfolds is lethal for any company, its shareholders, and its prospects for survival.

Law of the 21st-Century Business Jungle

It is now accepted that we should "say good-bye to the steady state." Nowhere is this more evident than in the developments of the US car industry. At the 2016 Consumer Electronics Show, in Las Vegas, most major car manufacturers made announcements about significant investments—in the billions—in revolutionary software, effectively trying to protect themselves against the likes of Google and other high-tech companies that are expected to be major disruptors in what is now positioned as the "personal mobility" industry. General Motors is investing US $500 million in LYFT, a San Francisco company that develops software for short-term car rental hubs so that drivers can work for Lyft (a competitor of Uber) without owning their own car.

Removing Blindfolds through Being a Judo Champion

Carrying on from the last example, "the idea is to leverage the force of the incoming, disruptive change in a way that actually strengthens [General Motors] and their company's position as a result." It seems that General Motors is simply trying to be a Judo Champion versus the perceived disruptive threat from Google and the likes of other high-tech companies.

The Message of Mavericks

Fundamentally, alert companies put up their own buoys so that they are never surprised by any global shockwave. In the banking sector, buoys are naturally set by closely following the regulators, who are increasingly demanding stricter regulatory measures and capital, on one side and by setting up close marketing follow-ups for the continuous erosion of the main earners for banks (transactional fees and loan interest income) from the naturally developing disintermediation of banks.

Application to My Career

I have been a personal eyewitness to the present struggles in the commercial and investment banking industry. Having worked for long periods in New York, Bahrain, London, Athens, Nicosia, and Cairo, and being CEO of several banks, I have had ample opportunity to see the six deadly blindfolds exhibited.

A classic example is increasing bank regulation, which has put inordinate burdens on smaller banks. In the United States, for instance, community banks find it very difficult to cope with the extra cost of banking regulations, even when they outsource most aspects of their back office. Some ignore this regulating trend and hope that their commercial business will bail them out, but most inevitably fail and are hastily sold off to larger competitors. Some small banks, on the other hand, are prescient enough to have buoys in place, to anticipate the future, and to find a friendly merger of their own.

With competition raging among banks in most markets, older fashion managements or even younger passionate but one-dimensional CEOs often fall into the traps of *We know what's best for the customer* or, worse, *dismissing competitors' success*. Not everyone is Steve Jobs, though, in anticipating future demand and client preferences. We therefore see many banks thrown onto the rocks and hastily merged into the hands of a competitor or taken over by governments themselves.

Advice to the Reader

The moral of this chapter is loud and clear. You must face your market with no self-imposed blindfolds. You must also have your own buoys in place so you can be alert, both individually and organizationally, to global shockwaves that may fundamentally affect your business.

However drastic it may sound, I sincerely believe that the banking industry as it is currently constituted—and as it is currently regulated—is facing its inevitable extinction. Three of the six deadly blindfolds that seem to be openly exhibited are arrogance, believing problems don't exist, and avoiding the unavoidable.

Do whatever it takes to ensure you never self-impose the six deadly blindfolds individually or organizationally!

About the Expert

Constantinos Loizides is currently the CEO of Piraeus Bank Egypt and Chairman of Piraeus Bank Cyprus.

He previously served as Vice Chairman and Managing Director of Hellenic Bank and as Managing Director of Bankers Trust Co. in New York, Bahrain, and London. Loizides was the head of the Middle East and North Africa Division for European Telecoms. He was also involved in European Capital Markets and Privatisations in Eastern Europe. Loizides serves on many boards of international organisations, including the International Chamber of Commerce in Paris, and in the past, as nonexecutive Chairman of Cyprus Airways.

Loizides holds a BSc from the Imperial College of Science and Technology, in London, and an MBA from MIT.

<><><><><><><><><><><><><><><><><><><><><><><><><><><><><><>

Chapter Three

THE REINVENTION FORMULA

AN ALGORITHM FOR QUANTUM INDIVIDUAL AND ORGANIZATIONAL CHANGE

"We're only at 1 percent of what's possible. Despite the faster change, we're still moving slow relative to the opportunities that we have."

—Larry Page

Recapturing the Magic and Profits through Reinvention

By 2007, Disney World seemed to be losing much of its magic. Parents were tired of high ticket prices, long lines, and complicated ticketing systems. Some families began to perfect the divide-and-conquer strategy. One tally had an enterprising family passing through Cinderella's Castle in the middle of the park almost twenty times each day in an effort to beat the crowds.

Also in evidence were a few questionable strategies to eliminate the complexity of visiting the Magic Kingdom.

Some wealthy parents hired disabled people with handicap scooters to pose as family members. This allowed their kids to jump to the front of the lines. Despite some of these black market guides costing upward of $130 an hour, one proud parent bragged to a reporter, "My daughter waited one minute to get on [the ride] 'It's a Small World,' while the other kids waited two and a half hours! It's just something you have to do these days at Disney if you have the money."

The Next Generation Experience Project

By 2008, CEO Bob Igor had seen enough. He realized he and Disney had to act. This led Igor to launch the most ambitious Disney project since the days of Walt.

This one-billion-dollar investment was code-named Next Generation Experience, and Igor told the initial project leadership team that the goal was to completely rethink the guest experience. Igor stressed that without challenging every assumption Disney held, Disney would likely miss out on the next generation of guests.

The team launched hard and fast. And Disney eventually gave the public a completely overhauled customer experience that seems to thrill guests once more.

The MagicBand

The visible product was a computer-like wristband called MagicBand. This innovation stored everything a guest might need digitally—park tickets, photos, coupons, monorail tickets, money, and ride turnstile passes. The guest experience was completely reimagined.

Consider the typical family that has built up an appetite during the morning and is ready for lunch. One of the parents simply orders food from the new mobile phone app and then heads to the Be Our Guest restaurant.

If you have a MagicBand, the host meets you as you walk into the restaurant and says, "Welcome, Tanner family!" Another hostess then takes over and says, "Please sit anywhere you like!" Neither mentions that the food will eventually find them. Soon, their hot food arrives exactly as ordered, delivered by a smiling young person pushing an ornately carved serving cart that resembles a display case in an old museum.

And just like that, the magic that Walt always wanted was built back into Disney World.

Reinvention Requires Systemic Change

Disney installed hundreds of thousands of short- and long-range sensors throughout the 27,000-acre property. Sensors allowed Disney to track guests as they navigated through the park. This had the benefit of creating a more efficient flow of visitors.

If one section of the park was overwhelmed with guests, operators could immediately disperse a character parade around the corner. A character like Goofy, with access to real-time guest information, could even whisper happy birthday to a child without prompting.

Although the final product was a simple, colorful, high-tech wristband, the changes behind the scene were hugely systemic. Departments that had never talked with each other before now had to be fully integrated. Staff behaviors and culture had to be changed. Virtually every process, system, and structure had to be realigned during this radical "pivot" to once again make Disney *the* premier theme park in the world.

Was Reinvention Worth It?

Were there difficulties during the multiyear transformation at Disney World? Certainly. With reinvention everything is on the table. It is the toughest of all changes. It challenges the status quo and those who protect it. It challenges the typical response, "That's just how we do things around here."

Disney's reinvention has made all the difference. Average wait times for entrance, food, and bathrooms are down thirty-three percent. They can now easily fit five thousand more guests per day into the park, drastically increasing revenue and profitability. The metric of "guests intending to return" is up sharply. The economic moat around Disney is back to a formidable size. They accelerated results by tackling massive change head on.

After the Next Generation Experience project team presented to Disney executives to get approval, Steve Jobs, who was unable to attend because of his late-stage cancer struggle, sent this message along: "I love what you guys are doing. You won't get everything right, but doing what you've been doing and believing that will be the model for the next twenty years is also not right."

Reinvention Defined

The Age of Disruption has changed the rules of the game. Constant reinvention may be exactly what is needed to maintain a strong trajectory of performance in the 21st century.

We define Reinvention as

"Quantum Individual and Organizational Change Accelerated."

What differentiates this definition from other change-oriented definitions is the use of two key words: "quantum" and "accelerated." These are must-have words if individuals and organizations are going to be able to align to the Law of the 21st-Century Business Jungle and the 21st-Century Competitiveness Cycle.

Quantum refers to the need for individuals and organizations to be prepared to make profound and deep changes when needed. *Accelerated* refers to the need for individuals and organizations to make major change happen much faster than what was required in the past.

THE PRINCIPLE OF ENERGY RELEASE

During change, there will be a natural energy release. The issue is how you funnel that energy, positively or negatively. Reinvention orchestrators design reinvention efforts to create, and leverage, positive energy release.

Having quality frameworks, processes, and tools to reinvent yourself and your organization will be a competitive advantage. This applies to Fortune 500 companies all the way down to street vendors in New York City and New Delhi. Even big government, sports franchises, and small city councils can improve their ability to make major change happen.

Three Degrees of Change

We suggest that there are three degrees of change that individuals and organizations can engage in when striving to improve performance:

- **Degree 1: Continuous improvement:** Consistently upgrading your ability to get results.

- **Degree 2: Renovation:** Performing a refresh in order to make a meaningful leap in performance.

- **Degree 3: Reinvention:** Totally rethinking your business and your ability to compete, perform, and drive results. Nothing is off the table in Reinvention.

This book primarily focuses on Degree 3: Reinvention. The principles we espouse, however, are also applicable to the first two degrees of change, just in smaller doses and with a narrower scope. The following tables better define the three degrees of change.

INDIVIDUAL CHANGE: THREE DEGREES

	Degree 1: Continuous Improvement	Degree 2: Renovation	Degree 3: Reinvention
Description	These professionals consistently upgrade their skills and knowledge within their current work discipline. Their goal is to maintain an upward trajectory in their career path. These people are satisfied with their work discipline and with the company they represent.	These professionals are ready to refresh their career by exploring new career opportunities or fields of expertise. This could be within the current company or at a different one. Renovation requires studying new work disciplines, acquiring new skills, and earnestly reaching out and leveraging their network.	These professionals are rethinking their career path and occupation, and want to make comprehensive change. Reinvention requires core changes in one's mind-set, skill set, tool set, and behavioral set. These individuals create a new personal brand. They are no longer emotionally controlled by their current work situation, but feel free to explore new possibilities.
Reasons for Change	They are motivated to further their career by delivering better results through updated skills and tools.	Sometimes uneasiness pushes these people to ask, "Will I be happy doing what I am doing in the future? Will I have made my highest contribution if I stay the course? Is there a potential threat to my current career path?" When the answers are "yes," then a renovation is likely needed.	People in this category find that their skills, résumé, and knowledge are outdated, and it is time to go back to the starting line. Others in this category might be financially secure, but want to reinvent themselves for the challenge and for greater career satisfaction. People in this group may also want to be in the forefront of a change that they sense is coming.
Difficulty	Low	Medium	High

ORGANIZATIONAL CHANGE: THREE DEGREES

	Degree 1: Continuous Improvement	Degree 2: Renovation	Degree 3: Reinvention
Description	These organizations invest in upgrades to processes, systems, knowledge, and skills each year in hopes of continuous incremental improvement.	These organizations seek to take their game to the next level and realize continuous improvement won't provide enough boost in performance. They aren't ready for a complete overhaul, but need to target several areas that are holding the company back.	These organizations have a strong need to rethink their entire business. Everything–strategy, processes, people, culture, product portfolio, brand image, and even sacred cows–is on the table.
Reasons for Change	These organizations seek to stay one step ahead of industry and market changes, and competitive movements.	These organizations' current performances and marketplace positions are unacceptable, and fine-tuning won't put them back into market leadership. The culture, leadership, and product portfolio may be stagnant and due for a shake-up.	These organizations are beginning to envision dire consequences if they don't do something. Other organizations have decided that being second or third year after year isn't acceptable.
Difficulty	Low	Medium	High

The Reinvention Formula: Addressing 3rd-Degree Change

We depict the Reinvention Formula as an algorithm. Our experience suggests that making quantum change isn't a random exercise. That would just create quantum confusion. Making quantum change entails following a high-level process and understanding that iterations must take place along the way. But certain steps usually precede other steps.

The best way to think about the Reinvention Formula is to view it as a high-level process flow. It shows all of the elements that must be addressed and suggests the order in which that should be done.

Master change agents use a blended combination of both art and science when bringing about powerful change. The Reinvention Formula is the "science" part of the equation, and the ten Powerful

Attributes of Reinventors, presented in Chapter Six, is the "art" portion. Making reinventive change happen requires applying both explicit-codifiable (science) and tacit-noncodifiable (art) knowledge.

The Reinvention Formula advocates that five crucial elements be addressed and mastered for quantum and effective change to happen:

- **Dissatisfaction (D):** Ensuring there is a strong and powerful internal felt need for change.

- **Focus (F):** Ensuring there is a compelling and articulated desired future state that generates forward movement and staying power.

- **Alignment (A):** Ensuring appropriate infrastructure is installed—processes, tools, structure, equipment, finances, systems—to enable flawless execution of the focus.

- **Execution (E):** Ensuring a comprehensive game plan with clear milestones is in place; installing a high-performance culture that executes well and fast.

- **Leadership (L):** Ensuring exceptional leadership (self-leadership for individuals; organizational leadership for organizations) is exhibited; ensuring the change quotient is in place and high accountability to the game plan.

These elements must outweigh the Cost of Change:

- **Cost of Change (C):** The true and perceived costs of change relative to the reinvention effort (physical, social, financial, emotional, and mental).

> ## THE REINVENTION FORMULA
>
> # REINVENTION
>
> # =
>
> # $(D \times F \times A \times E)L > C$
>
> (Dissatisfaction × Focus × Alignment × Execution) Leadership > Cost of Change

There are three major clusters that comprise the Reinvention Formula.

1. **Cluster #1: Change Quotient (D × F × A × E):** These are the four elements that bold choices must be made around to achieve the future desired state. They are bundled together because they must be tightly aligned.

2. **Cluster #2: Leadership (L):** Leadership is the single most important factor in the Reinvention Formula. We believe the saying, "Without leadership, everything else is just interesting." Without leadership making the right choices around the Change Quotient, and without Leadership ensuring forward momentum despite barriers and obstacles, the Change Quotient choices are just words on paper. Leadership truly is the Force Multiplier in a reinvention effort.

3. **Cluster #3: Cost of Change (C):** Disrupting the status quo can be painful. Reinvention is even more so, because the changes are bold in nature. Unless the combined forces of the Change Quotient (D × F × A × E) and Leadership (L) exceed the Cost of Change (C), then a reinvention effort is likely to fail. Costs can be physical, social, financial, and mental.

Defining the Sub-Components

The following is a detailed look into the sub-component of the Reinvention Formula with useful examples from our client work and studies.

Cluster #1: Change Quotient

D = Dissatisfaction

The first element in the Change Quotient is "dissatisfaction with the status quo." If an individual or organization hasn't internalized a strong, felt need for change, change will not occur. Addiction recovery programs teach that it is not enough for others to pressure an addict to change. The need must be self-generated. Dissatisfaction must be the first element addressed in any individual or organizational change effort.

Creating a Felt Need for Change
As internal consultants at a semiconductor manufacturing company, we learned important lessons.

The need to reinvent was high at this company. Stock had dropped from thirty dollars per share to three dollars per share, and the company was hemorrhaging money. We helped divisions and plants reengineer their operations and align to new strategies.

But there was a problem with the Analogue Division. This division had always been the darling and the moneymaker of the company, and was still doing better than the other divisions when we arrived.

The general manager of the Analogue Division held a meeting with his executive team to announce that the division was going to go through a redesign. But the pushback from his team was immediate, and the GM knew he could not move forward without their buy-in. So he came up with a solution.

He asked each executive team member to take the next 60 days to conduct an environmental scan. He told them he wanted to make sure they were aware of what was happening outside of the company. He put them into teams that looked at customer satisfaction, competitive movements, and industry trends.

And a funny thing happened. When the executives presented their findings, it was a different type of executive team. They were a humbled set of leaders. They discovered that they were actually number five in market share, down from number two, and dropping fast. They discovered new strategies of the competition. And customers gave them an earful. The executive team was now ready for a redesign.

F = Focus

Once an individual or organization is sufficiently dissatisfied with the current state, the first element to be addressed is Focus. This element creates great clarity on exactly what the future desired state should be. It also outlines the high-level strategies needed to accomplish the vision.

When your focus element is compelling, distractions and forces holding you to the status quo are suddenly minimized. A powerful focus is the most important element in maintaining momentum through the challenging times that are sure to come.

We Shall Never Surrender!

It was June 1940, and World War II was heating up. British troops had been evacuated from Dunkirk, France, in late May, and the Allies were in full retreat. Within a month, France would surrender to Nazi

Germany. It was common knowledge that Hitler would try to maintain momentum and immediately launch an all-out attack on Britain.

The mood in England was gloomy, among citizens and in Parlia-
ment. After taking over from Neville Chamberlain in May, Winston
Churchill gave three speeches in three weeks to rally England.

The speech he gave on June 4, 1940, in the House of Commons—
the third speech—was his finest one of all. Churchill roared,

> Even though large tracts of Europe and many old and famous
> States have fallen or may fall into the grip of the Gestapo and all
> the odious apparatus of Nazi rule, we shall not flag or fail. We
> shall go on to the end. We shall fight in France, we shall fight on
> the seas and oceans, we shall fight with growing confidence and
> growing strength in the air, we shall defend our island, whatever
> the cost may be. We shall fight on the beaches, we shall fight
> on the landing grounds, we shall fight in the fields and in the
> streets, we shall fight in the hills; we shall never surrender!

It was a completely different approach from that of his predeces-
sor, but one that was needed.

Afterward, a Labour Party minister wrote to Churchill and said,
"My dear Winston. That was worth one thousand guns and the
speeches of one thousand years."

Sure enough, just thirty-six days after Churchill's speech, the
German Luftwaffe began dropping bombs on England, and the Battle of Britain began. By late fall, fifty percent of London was completely flattened and almost forty thousand civilians had been killed.

But it was Churchill who "focused" a nation and created one
heart, one mind, and a laser resolve to never surrender. That is the
power of focus.

A = Alignment

Next, it is time to put in place processes, systems, activities, sched-
ules, technologies, and other infrastructure-type elements to enable

achievement of your chosen focus. It is about aligning all those things together tightly in a way that drives the needed and new behaviors.

Too Many Steps in Scotland

One of our projects took us to Scotland, where our task was to redesign a microchip manufacturing plant. We started by having the plant manager take us to where the raw materials first entered the plant and then show us how the product flowed through the facility. The idea was to see where and how far the materials traveled from start to finish.

We measured the distance that this entire journey took. We were shocked. The distance that the product traveled throughout the plant was 1.2 miles as it crisscrossed the plant dozens of times.

When the project was completed, the new manufacturing process required the product to travel only ten percent of the original distance. Imagine the waste of effort, time, and money that had accompanied its original manufacturing path! The plant manager had goals of manufacturing effectiveness and efficiency, but with such misaligned processes, structures, and systems, it was impossible to achieve those goals.

A Series of Base Camps

Alignment also means creating a roadmap to take you or your organization from point A to point B (focus). No one has ever climbed to the summit of Mount Everest on the Nepalese side without having made it to all five critical base camps.

Edmund Hillary, the first ever to climb Everest in 1953, was the genius behind the base camp system, which helped climbers to achieve greater success by focusing on only one base camp at a time, versus aiming right for the summit.

E = Execution

Reinvention eventually comes down to doing things that you've never done before in order to get results that are new and improved.

For individuals, it is all about new behaviors. For organizations, it is about culture.

For individuals and organizations, this often requires challenging current beliefs, assumptions, and worldviews that might get in the way of achieving the new goals.

Misalignment in Japan

One of our clients was the US Naval Shipyard Repair Facility in Yokusaka, Japan. The captain hailed from the United States and had every intention to do the very best job she could during her three-year stint. She loved the Japanese nationals who worked for her.

Early on, she decided to begin giving awards to the 1,600-person workforce (ninety percent Japanese and ten percent American) for stellar performance. She would do this publicly to show appreciation for the employees' contributions.

During the first award ceremony, she presented a prestigious award to one of the frontline Japanese workers. It was an award for individual excellence.

But a funny thing happened the following day. The employee never showed up for work. And then that absence turned into weeks.

Unable to make sense of this, the captain finally consulted one of her Japanese staff about the missing employee. He then taught her an unforgettable lesson: "In Japan, we never single out an individual. That is shameful. We believe we are all part of a larger whole and that one job is just as important as another. What you did with good intent embarrassed him so badly that he is considering quitting in disgrace. In Japan," he continued, "we are taught as children that the nail that stands out will get hammered down."

With this explanation, the captain's worldview on how best to motivate and reward Japanese employees was radically altered. Clearly, if she wanted to increase "execution" in the Japanese homeland, it would require a shift in her mind-set and behavioral set to focus not on the performance of an individual, but on the performance of the team.

Cluster #2: Leadership (L)

L = Leadership

We show the Leadership (L) element acting as a Force Multiplier to the Change Quotient in the Reinvention Formula (D × F × A × E). This is a hugely symbolic choice and one that is vital to understand. A Force Multiplier is defined as something that dramatically increases (hence multiplies) the total effectiveness of what it affects.

As the world continues to spin faster and faster, it will continue to throw off both issues and opportunities at a faster pace. Exceptional leaders will immediately recognize and act upon them. There is a premium on leadership like never before. We like to say "without leadership, nothing else really matters."

For reinvention to take place, there must be superior leadership. For individual reinvention, this would be symbolized as self-leadership. In organizational reinvention, it would be symbolized as team and organizational leadership.

Great leaders (Leader-Accelerators) blow life into both people and processes, whereas poor leaders (Leader-Decelerators) suck life out of everything they touch.

We know great leaders when we experience them. But have you ever thought about the importance of being a leader who creates willing followers?

Willing Followers

To determine a leader's effectiveness, the most important question we ask is this: "To what degree do people willingly follow you?" The critical word is *willingly*. It takes more than an impressive title to be a leader. Great leaders create willing followers based upon their moral character, not their management level.

When Mahatma Gandhi first began peacefully organizing Indian peasants, farmers, and urban laborers in the 1920s to 1940s to protest against the British government tax, discrimination, and imposed poverty policies, he had no positional authority. He was just a humble lawyer who saw a need and stepped up. And people willingly followed him en masse.

Powerful leaders with no moral authority gain followers through lies, threats, bribes, and promises. But their true influence is generally short-term.

The dictator is always overthrown.

Virtual and Flat Requires Persuasion
Our world has become less vertical and more flat. And it is certainly more virtual.

Country boundaries are less influential than they've ever been. In such a world, leadership that is vertical and power-based becomes less relevant. The key success factor, then, becomes the ability of the leader to persuade others to collaborate on a compelling vision.

The Arbinger Institute notes, "If you want to change another person, then give them someone different to respond to." Powerful advice. Putting a twist on this quote, we might say, "If you want to change yourself, give yourself someone different to respond to."

Your leadership is on display every day. How you show up as a leader to yourself and to others makes all the difference.

Cluster #3: Cost of Change (C)

C = Cost of Change

Change can be dreadfully challenging. Breakthroughs happen when we *break with* old forms of behavior, beliefs, processes, and anything else keeping us stuck in the status quo. And there is always a cost to doing so.

The last part of the Reinvention Formula stresses that the Cost of Change must be accounted for. It emphasizes that the Change Quotient (Dissatisfaction, Focus, Alignment, and Execution) multiplied by Leadership must be collectively more powerful than the Cost of Change. Costs of Change can be things such as finances, position, time, mental strain, social rearrangement, and reputation.

Losing Power Is a Deal Breaker

One of our oil and gas clients in Texas captures an interesting take on the Cost of Change.

Our project was ensuring that a new ERP system was fully accepted and used by the workforce. We formed a team of leaders and employees to help facilitate the project. One gentleman (a middle manager we'll call Sam) was included on the project team because he was highly influential, yet had a reputation for resisting new changes. If he bought in, we might be able to get some mileage from him in influencing others.

During one particular team meeting, we were discussing potential structural changes. When the discussion began focusing on his division, Sam immediately dug in his heels. He folded his arms across his broad chest and dared someone to knock the chip off his shoulder.

We asked him to share his feelings about the proposed changes in his division. He paused for a second, collected his thoughts, and then simply said, "I don't see myself changing much."

And that was that. His arms stayed folded on his chest, and there was silence in the room. Sam had essentially said, "Look, I'm willing to go along with all of your changes. But my position as a manager is very important to me. Losing my supervisor position is just too high a cost for me to accept."

Change Is Inevitable . . . Growth Is Optional: What's Your Position?

Forbes recently captured a powerful principle when thinking about going through major transformation:

> "Change is the new normal for leadership success, and all leaders must accept this fact. Leadership in the 21st century not only requires the ability to continuously manage crises and change— but also a circular vision to see around, beneath, and beyond the obvious in order to anticipate the unexpected before it hits you."

TRANSFORMING NASA'S KENNEDY SPACE CENTER

Putting the Reinvention Formula to the Test

By Dr. Phillip Meade, Division Chief, Spaceport,
NASA's Kennedy Space Center

In 2012, the Kennedy Space Center (KSC) was facing a critical need for Reinvention. I watched as a series of shockwaves rocked the space center to its core and left its standing as the nation's preeminent human launch site in question—and perhaps its very existence.

The twenty-year Shuttle program had been cancelled in order to free up budget to allow the creation of a new launch system capable of interplanetary exploration. However, in 2010 this replacement program was cancelled with little hint of a significant mission to replace it.

Additionally, new players to the space industry in the form of dot.com billionaires, such as Elon Musk, Jeff Bezos, and Richard Branson, were fundamentally changing the structure of the industry. These new competitors challenged the traditional standards and associated costs of access to low earth orbit. Their initial success allowed NASA to implement its strategy of commercializing access to the International Space Station and focus on its exploration mission.

I could see that the program would require only a fraction of the infrastructure and support that the Shuttle did. Additionally, exploration missions have fundamentally different operational profiles than missions to low earth orbit. With the closest planet being at least a 260-day journey one-way, the launch rate is significantly lower with little need for parallel processing capabilities.

We were left with a 140,000-acre launch site complete with two heavy-class launch pads, numerous world-class processing facilities, and a phenomenal support infrastructure that the new program neither needed nor could afford.

Reinvention was KSC's only hope for survival.

We **Scanned the External Environment**, and it revealed an opportunity to capitalize on the growth of the new entrants to the space industry. A possible win–win scenario existed where KSC could retain much of its valuable infrastructure and offset some of the fixed costs borne by its programs, while these new entrants could avoid the astronomically high initial investment costs of building their own launch infrastructure.

To do this, we would have to transform KSC from being primarily a government facility into a multi-user spaceport catering to NASA programs, other government entities, and commercial partners. To execute such a large reinvention effort, we had to employ the **Reinvention Formula**.

To make sure that senior leaders were clear about the **Dissatisfaction Level** with the status quo, a senior management retreat was held in which executives were painfully honest about what life at KSC would look like if no changes were made. These stark portraits were contrasted with various scenarios of a future KSC spaceport. The clear consensus coming out of this offsite was that doing nothing was not an option.

We then did significant work to help **Focus** ourselves around what the major strategies were that we were designing for. A 20-year spaceport master plan was developed which detailed future land use and laid out a plan for the use of existing facilities.

Alignment design choices were then made around the organizational structure. A directorate was created to focus on the creation of agreements with commercial partners to help the center achieve its vision for becoming a multi-user spaceport. As this directorate began having more and more success, another design change was made to create a directorate focused on implementing the agreements and integrating operations at the spaceport. We developed and modified numerous policies to accommodate the spaceport vision and allow the center to begin operating on a fundamentally different level.

(Continued)

We spent significant time ensuring the proper **Leader-Employee Behaviors** by educating employees on the goals and purpose of the spaceport vision. Numerous all-hand and town hall meetings with the center director were held so employees could hear the plans, learn about progress, and ask questions. I even facilitated focus group sessions to further gather employee feedback and provide an opportunity to educate.

Change leaders selected within the workforce have been pushing the boundaries and challenging the attitudes of other employees around being more flexible and conducive to commercial operations.

While work still remains, it is clear that we have made significant change in leader-employee behaviors in line with the spaceport goals.

Throughout our reinvention effort, the presence of **Exceptional Leadership** has been critical to ensuring success. Our leaders are not only adept at applying the Reinvention Formula, they are also incredibly resilient despite natural pushback.

We continue the process of reinvention. And we continue to iterate our strategies and design. But without a systemic framework such as the Reinvention Formula and Reinvention Roadmap, it is hard to imagine such a successful solution would have been realized.

Staking Out Your Highest and Best Use

Have you ever pondered on what you truly are the best at doing professionally? Have you written down what kind of "dent" you want to make in the universe before your career ends?

A recent thought leader suggested that today and in the past, individuals and companies aligned themselves primarily to "profit streams" such as retail, health care, finance and accounting, and manufacturing.

This thought leader submitted that future leaders and organizations that celebrate great success will be those that begin to align to "purpose streams." Purpose streams are defined by higher-cause areas such as global poverty, global education, getting technology to every human, green energy, diversity, and so forth.

Working for *Purpose* versus *Profit*

Fast Company recently said this in a high-profile article: "Starting and surviving in today's economy is hard, but the companies that figure it out have something in common: the pursuit of purpose, alongside the pursuit of profit. A purpose mobilizes people in a way that pursuing profits alone never will. For a company to thrive, it needs to infuse its purpose in all that it does."

We agree. The Millennials are very clear that they want to make an impact on the world and are constantly in search for a higher purpose to link to. Millennials are showing with their feet that working for a *purpose* rather than working for *profit* is what keeps them coming back to work, day after day, fully energized.

Research shows that Millennials are more loyal to a *job* than to an *employer*. They observed the working relationship their parents had with their employers, and seem to adhere to a new principle: "Why be loyal to a company that doesn't return the same loyalty when the chips are down?"

This search for meaning and purpose is on the agendas of most Millennials in the Western world and increasingly in the developing economies.

There seem to be two types of organizations that embrace being "purpose-driven" versus "profit-driven": those that begin as purpose-driven companies and those traditional profit-driven companies that are developing corporate responsibility strategies tied into a higher purpose. The idea is to "do well by doing good."

The following chart is based upon a few examples from *Fortune* magazine's list of Change the World Companies. Notice that fifty percent are new companies while fifty percent are older companies that are aligning themselves to a socially responsible, purpose-driven industry.

We think it likely that we will see a pendulum shift within big companies over the next decade in the percentage purpose-driven versus percentage profit-driven ratio. The answer in the future seems to be a nice mix of purpose-driven AND profit-driven.

Industry	Purpose-Driven Examples
Telecommunications	**Vodafone**–Connecting the unbanked masses to the global economy. **Impact**: Now 17 million people are using M-Pesa, which allows people with smartphones but no bank accounts to save and transfer money, receive pensions, and pay bills.
Technology	**Cisco Systems**–Training a tech workforce that could lift up the Middle East. **Impact**: The Israeli office has an outsourcing program that finds young talent in Palestinian territories. The IT outsource sector has grown 64 percent and provides Cisco a broader, deeper, and cheaper pool of workers.
Food	**Danone**–Nutrition, tailored to those who need it most. **Impact**: Danone abandoned the junk food business to pursue ways to feed the poor. In Bangladesh, children eat 600,000 servings of Shokti-Doi, a nutrient rich yogurt, every day.
Homebuilding	**Cemex**–Homes for prices even the poor can afford. **Impact**: In exchange for fixed, regular payments, Cemex will send building materials and technical support to do-it-yourselfers in Latin America. Over 500,000 families have been able to build their own homes.
Transportation	**BYD**–Their better bus could solve a smog crisis. **Impact**: Half of the world's air pollution comes from transportation sources, so this Chinese company has invented buses that can run a full day just on batteries.

It is important that readers who feel the need to reinvent understand the trend toward purpose-driven industries. It is never too late to notice important disruptive trends and make your impact.

The Copernican Revolution in Management

Nicolaus Copernicus thought big. This German mathematician and astronomer of the 16th century was an out-of-the-box thinker. The Copernican Revolution describes the massive paradigm shift and worldview change Copernicus placed upon the world and society.

This paradigm shift challenged the view that the Sun revolved around the stationary "center of the universe"—the Earth—to the view that the Earth is one of several planets revolving around the Sun.

At first, this new view of things seemed to be just a mathematical exercise, and it was easily accepted. But when this new view of things began challenging the concept of religion, societal structures, and such, the Copernican Revolution became uncomfortable as it challenged the long-held status quo.

Author Thomas Kuhn coined the term "The Copernican Revolution in Management" to describe the new paradigm shifts that are happening within our new business environment.

He specifically highlights the 20th-century view that customers revolve around the stationary "center of the universe," or the value chain of the organization, to the better view that the company is one of many organizations revolving around the customer. The organization survives and thrives only so long as it is agile enough to meet the customer's shifting needs and desires.

We want to continue to stress the importance of the new Law of the 21st-Century Business Jungle we proposed in Chapter Two. What is the paradigm shift? That being able to radically reinvent on a dime is no longer a "nice to have." It will be table stakes and, in the future, simply the price of entering the game.

Now Is the Time to Think Big

Consider one of our favorite company mantras that we first heard uttered by Zappos cofounder Tony Hsieh. We have it plastered on our office wall. It simply, but very powerfully, says,

Whatever you're thinking, think bigger!

Expert Insight: Dr. Phillip Meade

As the authors of the *Forbes* article astutely point out, "The Age of Disruption has changed the rules of the game. . . . Change is the new normal for leadership success, and all leaders must accept this fact."

The ability to lead transformational change is now an imperative for continued success. This is a scary fact, given the current inability of most organizations to do so. A recent article in *Harvard Business Review* restated a well-known—if painful—statistic: only thirty percent of transformational change efforts are successful, regardless of industry. Those are pretty bad odds. Fortunately, as the authors also point out, "making quantum change isn't a random exercise."

The Reinvention Formula presented in this chapter provides an excellent process for individuals and organizations to follow. The true power of this formula is the fact that it addresses the total system. Organizations often address one or two components while neglecting others and then wonder why they don't see the results they desire. This is like including only part of the ingredients in a recipe and wondering why it doesn't taste right.

The power of this chapter is that it clearly defines the critical ingredients for reinvention to happen fast and proactively.

Key Insights

The greatest takeaways for me from this chapter are below.

Alignment and Taking a Systems Approach to Reinvention
Without viewing the total system that you are trying to change and understanding the interactions of each component, you can never truly hope to effect lasting change.

All Change Is Not Created Equal
There are three distinct types of change, and failing to recognize which type you are dealing with can create unnecessary costs and can lead to failure.

Leadership Is the Key
No matter how well you engineer the reinvention effort, its success ultimately rests on the quality of leadership. Leaders truly are the force multipliers. It is essential to have leaders who people willingly follow during a reinvention effort.

Purpose Captures Hearts
Clearly, organizations must make a profit to enable them to achieve their mission. But more and more, employees want to leave a mark and contribute to something greater than themselves. Emphasizing the true, noble purpose of the organization can pay dividends.

Don't Discount the Cost of Change; Copernican Revolutions Are Relative
Any reinvention effort will result in a Copernican revolution for some constituents. Failing to see the change from their viewpoint and to adequately calculate the true cost of the paradigm shift they must undergo will create significant barriers to success. It will be tempting to discount this cost, but don't do it.

Application to My Career

I have had the opportunity to lead several reinvention efforts in my career. Among the most dramatic was leading the cultural and organizational change at Kennedy Space Center (KSC) following the *Columbia* space shuttle accident. Our goal was to ensure the safety and operations of future shuttle missions. We were very concerned about preventing a similar accident. We needed to reconnect leaders and employees to the true purpose of KSC and NASA.

To successfully lead a cultural change of this magnitude—and to do so under the microscope that we were under—required a world-class change process. Like the Reinvention Formula states, it was necessary for KSC to recognize the systemic nature of the organization. As the CAIB (*Columbia* Accident Investigation Board) reported, it wasn't just the foam that hit the wing that caused the accident. It was the leadership and organizational culture of NASA at the time. We had to ensure there was sufficient dissatisfaction with the status quo before moving forward. We had to communicate a better future state, align the organizational infrastructure, and ultimately ensure that these new changes drove positive behavioral change.

Advice to the Reader

I suggest you develop your own capability to take a systems approach to reinvention. Organizations are complex, adaptive systems, where coupling and feedback between the components create unexpected responses and resistance to change. Just think about the last time you tried to implement any stand-alone policy!

Because of this, it is absolutely critical to understand the whole system. How do its pieces work together to produce overall performance? Only by intentionally aligning the total system to the new behaviors and outcomes can reinvention success be achieved. If you doubt this, reread the case study of Disney's Next Generation Experience project.

Reinvention isn't easy, but it is possible. Hang in there, and stay committed to achieving your goal. Help is available, and this chapter provides a great overview of the macro-level process and formula required for success.

About the Expert

Dr. Phillip T. Meade is the Division Chief for the Spaceport Management and Integration Division at NASA, Kennedy Space Center. His division helped KSC become a multiuser spaceport, with a broad base of commercial users, in addition to the traditional NASA program work. The goal is to leverage common architecture, processes, operations, and infrastructure to reduce costs and time-to-market for customers.

Meade has led major reinvention efforts within NASA throughout his career from various positions and has consulted on many more. He has two patents to his name and received both the NASA Exceptional Achievement Medal and the NASA Silver Achievement Medal.

Meade has a BS in electrical engineering, an MS in engineering management, and a PhD in industrial engineering.

Chapter Four

<><><><><><><><><><><><><><><><><><><><><><><><><>

ASSESSING YOUR NEED
FOR REINVENTION

USING EVALUATION CRITERIA TO
DETERMINE THE BEST PATH FORWARD

"Expect the unexpected. And, whenever possible, be the unexpected."

—*Lynda Barry*

Black Gold in Dubai

The question on Sheikh Rashid's mind in 1966 was, "What should we do next economically when our oil reserves disappear?" Black gold had just been discovered in his emirate of Dubai.

The good news was obvious. As the world became more oil dependent, oil would be one of Dubai's most valuable exports. But this news also contained a challenge. Dubai's oil reserves were finite compared with those of its Middle Eastern neighbors. Estimates suggested that Dubai had approximately sixty years before all its oil reserves would be completely depleted.

Dubai lies directly on the Persian Gulf within the Arabian Desert region. Much of Dubai is topographically challenged because the vast majority of the land is of sandy desert origin. The country averages only fifty-two feet above sea level, and there are only about three and a half inches of rainfall each year. And temperatures in the summer months climb to well over one hundred degrees Fahrenheit.

Because of the lack of diversity in the geography and weather, Dubai's economy had always been small and was mainly focused on trade with other surrounding nations, primarily Iran.

But Sheikh Rashid was a rare visionary. He had a natural disposition toward long-term thinking and doing what was best for future generations. Even with nearly six decades of oil reserves still in the ground, in 1966, Sheikh Rashid set out to reinvent his country's economy.

A Visionary Reinventing the Future

Once oil revenues began materializing in 1969, Sheikh Rashid launched his ambitious plan of diversified growth.

Dubai's first major project was the construction of the deepwater harbor, Port Rashid. Using a British company as the contractor, Sheikh Rashid built a world-class port that could accommodate sixteen ships at one time. Within a decade, the number rose to thirty-two. The project was an incredible success, with shipping customers waiting in line to access the new facilities.

From there, he launched new projects to create modern infrastructure, including roads, bridges, schools, and hospitals. Oil revenues funded all this. By 1975, the nation's population had grown by three hundred percent.

And then Sheikh Rashid's big vision came online. The endgame was to turn Dubai into a world destination that tourists and businesses flocked to. This would bring outside investment, steady employment, and wealth. And, if done well, it would eventually create a wealthy Dubai independent of oil revenues.

Over time, Sheikh Rashid created a culture within his emirate of growth, diversification, and optimism.

From Small Trading Port to the Manhattan of the Middle East

In less than fifty-five years, Dubai has become the seventh most visited city in the world, with the fastest growth rate at 10.7 percent per annum. In 2015 alone, Dubai accommodated more than fifteen million tourists.

Dubai's lure for tourists is based mainly on shopping. The city has been called the "shopping capital of the Middle East." Dubai alone has more than seventy shopping centers.

Dubai's GDP is now at an amazing $107 billion, with less than 5 percent of revenues coming from oil exports. The top industries in terms of gross domestic product are aviation and tourism (30 percent), real estate and construction (22.6 percent), trade (16 percent), and financial services (11 percent).

The Palm Islands of Dubai are the largest artificial islands in the world and can be seen from the moon. Upon completion, the islands will support 500,000 people and will have two thousand villas, forty luxury hotels, shopping centers, movie theaters, restaurants, and a lot of resort features.

When it comes to reinvention, Sheikh Rashid's visionary approach is the gold standard. In the Age of Disruption, both individuals and organizations must view the value of their resources, strategies, and skills as finite and subject to change or even elimination. Like the Sheikh, we all must continue to plan the next version of our careers or organizations.

Confronting the Brutal Facts

In his seminal book *Good to Great: Why Some Companies Make the Leap . . . and Others Don't,* Jim Collins studied eleven companies that went from "good" to "great" and sustained that performance for at least fifteen years. Collins identified several factors that each company shared.

A key finding was that all eleven companies had a bias toward "confronting the brutal facts," rather than quietly brushing them under the carpet. In the same way that Sheikh Rashid confronted the brutal fact that his country's oil reserves were finite, these companies recognized that they could make significant improvements only after they embraced the full truth of their situation. They understood that you absolutely cannot make a series of good decisions without first confronting the brutal facts. As a result, these companies emerged from adversity even stronger than before.

It is quite easy to find examples of individuals and organizations that launched radical change because they had to. It is a bit more challenging to find examples like Sheikh Rashid of Dubai who had the foresight to reinvent before there was "dissatisfaction with the status quo."

The culmination of this brutal facts principle is what Collins calls the "Stockdale Paradox." The principle states the following:

It is vital to retain absolute faith that you can and will prevail in the end, regardless of the difficulties, and at the same time confront the most brutal facts of your current reality, whatever they might be.

What about you? How about the team or organization you associate with? Or the leaders you team up with? Is there a willingness to gather the facts and then confront the most brutal ones in an honest and urgent way?

Evaluations to Help You Assess Reinvention Needs

We've created two reinvention evaluations to help you get a sense of your current need for substantial change in your professional life or in your organizational realm. The first is for individuals, and the second is for organizations.

Both surveys are simple and straightforward, and each uses ten criteria to help you in your evaluation.

In both cases, please use a rating scale of 1 to 10 (1 = Do not agree; 5 = Moderately agree; 10 = Completely agree) to rate to each item.

Individual Reinvention Evaluation	Your Rating
1. Career satisfaction: You love your career and find great satisfaction in what you do.	
2. Skill proficiency: You are deeply knowledgeable and skilled at what you do.	
3. Contribution: You are making a rewarding and fulfilling contribution in your current role.	
4. Intellectual stimulation: Your mind is consistently challenged to learn new things.	
5. Financial satisfaction: You are happy with your total compensation and benefits.	
6. Career mobility: You see opportunities to move upward or horizontally in the future.	
7. Relationships: Your relationships at work energize you and are gratifying.	
8. Job security: You have job security in your current employment.	
9. Technology agility: You use technology to further your career and to network.	
10. Entrepreneurship: You are able to unleash your entrepreneurial spirit in your current job.	
Total Points	

After completing the individual evaluation, total your score and compare it with the following scoring legend for insight and guidance on the current state of your professional career.

0–69	You are a strong candidate for reinvention. Step up and take the challenge!
70–84	You are on the fence. Your performance and morale are likely stagnant or slipping. Consider changing (reinventing) before you have to!
85–100	Your need for reinvention is minimal. You simply need to make a few tweaks and refinements to your current career to stay relevant. But don't wait!

Organizational Reinvention Evaluation	Your Rating
1. Revenue growth: My organization is experiencing strong revenue growth.	
2. Profitability: My organization is making a healthy profit.	
3. Competitive position: My organization is always one step ahead of the competition.	
4. Customer satisfaction: My organization's customers are very satisfied.	
5. Cultural vibrancy: My organization's culture encourages employees' high performance.	
6. Technology agility: My organization applies technology to create a competitive advantage.	
7. Employee engagement: My organization's employees are highly engaged.	
8. Innovation: My organization creates innovation in our products, services, and processes.	
9. Learning agility: My organization is constantly learning and improving performance.	
10. Leadership: My organization exhibits world-class leadership.	
Total Points	

After completing the organization evaluation, total your score and compare it with the following scoring legend for insight and guidance on the current state of your organization's health.

0–69 Your organization is a strong candidate for reinvention. Step up as a leader and begin the discussion with your peers. Be proactive in every way!

70–84 Your organization is walking a fine line. Its performance is most likely less than desirable and heading in the wrong direction. Consider reinventing before you are forced to.

85–100 Your organization's need for reinvention is minimal. Most likely, you could use a continuous improvement process. But don't wait!

Acting on the Results of Your Reinvention Evaluations

We hope the evaluation exercises provided compelling insights into the current state of your professional and organizational health. No matter what the score, we suggest that you share your results with either a significant other, or significant others, for three reasons.

First, sharing your total and individual item scores with others can provide a reality check. Confidence can come from getting the okay from others that you are seeing things the way they really are.

Second, especially when talking about the organizational reinvention evaluation, this is a great opportunity to have your leadership team fill out this survey individually in a leadership team meeting, report their scores and reasons why, and then see to what extent the team is unified in their responses.

It is our experience that individuals on even the highest-performing leadership teams are surprisingly varied in their responses. Great insights can result from these discussions. Many teams agree to take this evaluation at least semiannually as a way of welcoming the brutal facts and addressing them proactively.

Lastly, compelling research shows that one of the most important factors of success among individuals tackling quantum change is to have the constant support of a significant other. When others know the challenge you are attempting, and your goal is out in the open, there is a significantly higher level of accountability and feeling of support during sure-to-come challenging times when you are slugging it out in the trenches.

THE PRINCIPLE OF NEMESIS

Find a good thing and count on this. A nemesis will appear. Nothing good lasts forever because others will want to share it.

The Blind Leading the Blind

If you are like us, it is tough to beat the embarrassment quotient when someone you know says something like this to you: "My friend, I just need to be honest with you. When you do [xyz], it not only drives me crazy, but it also drives others crazy. Can you work on that?"

But the embarrassment quotient doubles if you actually find yourself at a loss from the feedback because you never realized you were exhibiting such irritating behavior. And then you naturally wonder if you have other behaviors that you aren't aware of that are driving others crazy!

We call these types of behaviors—those we are completely unaware of—*Blind Spots*. This comes from the Johari Window model, created in 1955 by psychologists Joseph Luft and Harrington Ingham; it's a tool that has been used for decades by business leaders, executive coaches, and managers.

JOHARI WINDOW

	Known to Self	Not Known to Self
Known to Others	1. Public Self	4. Blind Spot
Not Known to Others	2. Private Self	3. Unknown

The robust way to use this model is to give the person being coached and evaluated a list of fifty-five adjectives and have them pick upward of ten that they believe accurately describe their personality. This person's peers are then given the same fifty-five words and asked to choose the ten adjectives they feel accurately describe their peer. These adjectives are then mapped onto the Johari Window grid to see the differences and prompt a discussion around self-awareness.

A House with Four Rooms

The philosopher Charles Handy calls the Johari model the "house with four rooms." Room one is the part of ourselves that we see and others see. Room two is our private space, which we know about but keep from others. Room three is the most mysterious room in that neither we nor others see the unconscious or subconscious part of us. Room four contains the aspects others see in us but of which we are unaware.

We generally use this model with clients as a conceptual framework to give us common and compelling language to talk about self-awareness, either individually or organizationally. It truly is amazing how much this model creates new awareness with individuals, teams, and organizations as they humbly evaluate their strengths, weaknesses, and impact on others—sometimes for the first time.

We suggest that once you have co-opted someone, or many others, to provide their evaluation of the Reinvention Formula themselves, you map the differences in answers onto the Johari Window grid to determine your current level of self-awareness or organizational awareness.

Viewing Feedback as a Gift: An Author's Personal Experience

Asking people to provide their reinvention evaluation and scoring of you or your organization is essentially asking for feedback. And personal or organizational feedback is rarely requested proactively. One of the authors of this book—to remain unnamed—got to feel the effects of feedback up close. This is the story:

"Early in my career, while working at a personal productivity and leadership firm, I was promoted to a new leadership role. I had been heavily recruited for the role, and I felt quite confident when I arrived at work on that first day. My direct supervisor suggested that I immediately take the firm's premier and well-known 360-degree feedback survey to familiarize myself with the instrument and methodology behind it. Or so I thought. It would be the first time I had ever received feedback from important others in my work environment.

"Suffice it to say, it was both a new and challenging learning experience. All 360-degree feedback instruments reported a person's strengths and weaknesses in their full glory and detail. It was painful to read through the lower scores on several of the items—and reading through the comments from coworkers was also painful. It was soon apparent that I had several blind spots to explore more fully.

"But over the years, I learned to view feedback as the breakfast of champions. Who wants to find out later in their career that they had been exhibiting a blind behavior, but no one had the courage to tell them?"

Just as receiving feedback at an individual level is critical for growth and renewal, it is also important for organizations to seek out and embrace feedback. This often comes from employees, customers, suppliers, shareholders, and other stakeholders.

One airline company that we know of actually views mishaps with customers as great opportunities to increase customer loyalty. The company trains its employees to wow the angry customer with innovative ways to take care of their problems.

TAYLOR'S FEEDBACK AND APPLE'S RESPONSE

Apple's new service in 2015, Apple Music, offered a simple proposition: for a monthly subscription fee, Apple would give you access to a library of more than thirty million song tracks. You could listen and explore to your heart's content, and you could take the music wherever you go. And it was all cloud-based.

Apple proposed to customers an initial three-month experience free of charge, to just try it out. And Apple let all music artists know they, too, wouldn't be paid royalties during those three months.

That is, until Taylor Swift wrote an open letter to CEO Tim Cook. Taylor wrote:

"I'm sure you are aware that Apple Music will be offering customers a free three-month trial to anyone who signs up for the service. I'm not sure you know that Apple Music will not be paying writers, producers, or artists for those three months. I find it shocking, disappointing, and completely unlike this historically progressive and generous company."

Within just a few hours after the note went public, Apple replied in this way: "We agree with you, Taylor. Thanks."

There might be just a handful of companies in the world who would have responded to this so quickly and in such a manner. And, in this case, it happened to be the world's most valuable company. No wonder this company continues to put customers and stakeholders first and reaps the benefits on the stock exchange.

Are You at a Crossroads?

The fossil fuel industry seems to be at a crossroads. Oil and gas giants continue to reap incredible profits from selling their traditional products. But as world leaders continue to meet for climate talks, and the bad news about global warming continues to pour in, the future of the fossil fuel industries seems to hang in the balance. An industry leader spoke with the *Huffington Post*:

> "We are going to look back at some point in the future and see 2015 as a real turning point for the industry," Andrew Logan, director of [the] oil and gas program at the sustainable business nonprofit Ceres, told the *Huffington Post*. "Either companies will see the writing on the wall and realize that their business-as-usual approach is a fool's errand—that'd be the optimistic outcome—or they [end] up doubling down on the business-as-usual approach and end up sowing the seeds of their own financial demise down the road."

Is your organization or career at a crossroads? Or can you clearly see the fork-in-the-road sign up ahead?

Now might be the time to reinvent.

Maybe Catherine Fake, a cofounder of Flickr, was onto something when she observed: "So often people are working hard at the wrong thing. Working on the right thing is probably more important than working hard."

What is your right thing?

Expert Insight: Claudio Fernández-Aráoz

Having personally assessed some twenty thousand executives throughout my career, I am in complete agreement with the authors on the need for individuals and organizations to engage in a rigorous assessment on the need for reinvention. Both assessments presented in the chapter are comprehensive and straightforward and seem to address all of the key metrics that would tell you whether major change is needed.

I found this chapter invaluable for any geography, as a very useful and fully practical assessment of our need for individual and organizational reinvention.

Key Insights

The most important chapter insights for me were the following:

Confronting the Brutal Facts

While working for McKinsey & Company early in my career, I was amazed to watch how a disciplined company review helped spot unique opportunities and threats in any industry. As a search consultant, I realized how a clever discussion with professionals could help executives perceive not just wake-up calls but even fire alarms! *Always check where you stand and where you are heading with relevant discussion partners.*

The Critical Truth about the Johari Window

As an expert in assessments, I still trust a candidate's references more than how the candidates evaluate themselves. Although we seem to be quite blind to inadequacies, others see us much more objectively. Blind spots are invaluable treasures! *Develop the habit of proactively seeking feedback from the most relevant sources.* Do this after every project or at periodic intervals at least twice a year.

Acting on Feedback

We all know the problem of New Year resolutions: it is as easy to make them as it is to give up on them. Once you gather any useful feedback, be specific about the change you will embark on, and then *make sure you go public with your commitment*; this will help you reconfirm the appropriateness of your change game plan, as well as your disciplined execution and follow-up strategies.

Discovering Your Right Thing

The most effective leadership transformations I've seen had a very narrow but incredibly precise laser focus. When helping leaders develop, I used to help them set several change objectives per year. These days, I usually help them focus on just one key priority and carefully put together an effective change plan. The impact over time of their personal or organizational transformation becomes much more powerful and sustainable.

Application to My Career

I was born and raised in Argentina, a place within Latin America where "even the past is unpredictable!" During the crisis of 2001–2002, the country had five presidents in twelve days, its GDP went down by 30 percent, and there was a 300-percent devaluation of our currency.

Unfortunately, in the Age of Disruption so clearly articulated in this book, the whole world has become—and will remain—significantly "Latin-Americanized," where increased volatility and disruption will become the new global normal.

Harvard Business Review produced their first ranking of the best CEOs in the world (considering their value creation in absolute terms and also adjusted by industry and country), and they were surprised to find that Latin America had a disproportionate representation of top leaders at both extremes of the ranking. Many Latin American CEOs had been unable to deal with the massive volatility, unpredictability, and chaos in the region, leading to massive value destruction and personal failure. Others, however, were able to masterfully navigate the troubled waters, reinvent, and achieve amazing results compared with their counterparts in less-volatile regions.

Advice to the Reader

Disruption is a wonderful opportunity for those who properly anticipate and prepare for whatever the world may throw at them. But it can also be a lethal threat for the unprepared.

Professional success increasingly favors the leaders who display a combination of four key hallmarks: curiosity, insight, engagement, and determination. Curiosity is the most important indicator, and it includes as one of its most significant behavioral indicators the ability to proactively seek feedback and act on it.

If you seriously engage in the feedback proposed in this chapter and diligently work with the roadmap and accelerators presented in the next two chapters, you will without question drastically increase your chances of surviving—and even thriving—in our fascinating world.

Having worked on hundreds of development initiatives, I can only reinforce the crucial need for reliable feedback in order to identify inevitable blind spots.

About the Expert

Claudio Fernández-Aráoz is a senior advisor at the leading executive search firm Egon Zehnder and a former member of its global executive committee. He previously worked for McKinsey & Company.

Fernández-Aráoz is a global expert on hiring, promotions, and leadership development and a frequent speaker at major business gatherings. His advice has been sought by the CEOs of several of the world's largest companies and governments. He is a regular lecturer at Harvard Business School and a frequent contributor to HBR.org. He is the author of *It's Not the How or the What but the Who* (Harvard Business Review Press, 2014), winner of the Gold Axiom Award for the best human resources book published in English globally, and of *Great People Decisions* (Wiley, 2007), which has 15 international editions.

Fernández-Aráoz holds an MBA from Stanford University.

Chapter Five

◇◇◇◇◇◇◇◇◇◇◇◇◇◇◇◇◇◇◇◇◇◇◇◇◇◇◇◇◇◇◇◇◇◇◇◇

THE REINVENTION ROADMAP

DESIGNING INDIVIDUALS AND ORGANIZATIONS FOR HIGH PERFORMANCE

"The common question that gets asked in business is 'Why?'
That's a good question, but an equally valid one is 'Why not?'"

—Jeff Bezos

Poor Results Are No Accident

One of our favorite client projects involved the largest private home-builder in the United States. This company was dissatisfied with its current customer-satisfaction results and approached us about redesigning its entire customer experience.

Like all our organizational projects, we began by forming several environmental scan teams composed of the company's employees and leaders who were involved in the home-building process in various capacities.

These teams talked to current customers, examined competitors' processes, visited companies outside the home-building industry for great ideas, and completed a detailed analysis of their company's current home-building process to identify what might be disappointing their customer base.

Environmental Scan Findings

The teams presented their findings to the project's steering committee. After summarizing the core themes from all the findings after all the presentations, both the presenters and listeners had an eye-opening experience. Heads were nodding as they began to understand that these unsatisfactory results were no accident. In fact, their customers were getting the exact experience that the company—intentionally or unintentionally—had designed for them.

Some of the larger findings were as follows:

- **No clear, integrated, and seamless process for customers to follow:** Customers were navigating through four disconnected functions: sales, design, production, and customer warranty.

- **No ownership or accountability:** No one in the company was responsible for the overall customer experience. No one was held accountable to clear performance metrics.

- **No company-wide building standards:** A customer's experience depended upon which general manager (GM) was assigned to his or her project. That was based on the location of the new home. Thus, a home's building standards depended upon how its GM had learned the trade from his or her previous employer.

- **No formalized customer touch points:** Unless a customer contacted the GM with complaints or questions, customers heard from the company only on a random, as-needed basis throughout the six-month home-building process.

- **Employee reward systems focused on profit and speed:** Employees working within the home-building process were generally rewarded on final results, which were a combination of high speed and low cost.

- **Unclear decision-making authority in solving customer problems:** Employees working directly with a customer were unsure as to what level of authority they had to provide on-the-spot solutions to customer problems.

Key Principle of High Performance

We then taught the client the most powerful principle behind building high-performance organizations and having a high-performance career.

Organizations and individuals are perfectly designed to get the results that they get.

The company's customer-satisfaction results were simply the outcome of how they chose to—or chose not to—structure their overall organization. We stressed that organizational results were rarely the product of happenstance or bad luck.

It was a major aha moment for the leadership team.

We explained that the good news was the same principle of "perfectly designed" could apply as they made new choices going forward. They could make new choices that aligned with exceeding customer expectations.

Using our Reinvention Roadmap, this large national home-builder designed a revolutionary customer experience process that became ranked the best in the industry. The customer experience was based on touch points and moments of truth. They were able to win the JD Power Award for best customer experience over the next two years. They were now getting the results they designed for—only this time, they were happy with them.

Master Physician and Systems Thinker

A Systems Thinker understands that most issues we confront are part of a larger whole.

Systems are composed of interrelated parts and components. Systems in nature include ecosystems, ocean currents, climate, and the solar system. Systems that humans have designed include airplanes, technologies, government agencies, manufacturing processes, and automobiles.

Dr. Craig Buhler has an impressive reputation. We know because he has treated us for various maladies, and we were amazed at the results.

For twenty-six years he served as a team physician for the Utah Jazz NBA basketball team. During his tenure he helped the Jazz achieve the lowest "player-missed games due to injury rate" in the NBA. All-Star point guard John Stockton missed only twenty-two games in his 1,504 game career. All-Star Karl Malone missed just ten games in his eighteen-year career. Today, Dr. Buhler treats elite athletes from around the world.

Buhler stands out from his peers because of his reliance on systems thinking. He views and treats the body as an overall system composed of thousands of parts. To work properly, every part must be aligned and in sync with other parts. When a patient shows up and explains the problems he or she is experiencing, Buhler begins thinking about potential root causes that bought about the appearance of the symptoms.

On the walls of his office, Dr. Buhler lists the most important guiding principles that he adheres to when working with patients. Note the systems thinking associated with the language.

- **Principle 1:** Our bodies are perfectly designed to produce the experience we get.

- **Principle 2:** We attempt to define the root cause of the problem rather than merely treat the symptom.

- **Principle 3:** There are always reasons for symptoms. Ignore them long enough, and disease and injury will be the result.

- **Principle 4:** Treating symptoms with unnecessary medications, drugs, and surgeries is in essence telling the body to be quiet.

- **Principle 5:** Pain and dysfunction are the result of the body modifying itself from its innate design. Modifications are due to an accumulation of imbalances caused by trauma and overload to your body's system.

Buhler's approach—and his success rate—confirms that even with our bodies, we are perfectly designed to get the results we get. Systems thinking is critical when reinventing individual careers and organizational performance.

Reinvention Formula versus Reinvention Roadmap

In Chapter Three, we introduced you to the Reinvention Formula. In this chapter, we explain how to implement that formula using the Reinvention Roadmap. The following chart details the key differences between the two.

	Definition and Purpose
Reinvention Formula	The purpose of the Reinvention Formula is to provide a high-level conceptual process for Reinvention. It is shown as an algorithm and introduces the "big five" elements that need to be addressed during Reinvention. The Reinvention Formula can be used as a visual flowchart rather than an implementation framework.
Reinvention Roadmap	The Reinvention Roadmap is a detailed and comprehensive translation of the Reinvention Formula. This framework is a working model that is used as an implementation template when doing Reinvention. The model actually guides you through linear steps of Reinvention and helps you iterate your reinvention game plan until you have designed your organization optimally.

The Reinvention Roadmap

The Reinvention Roadmap is meant to help you put the Reinvention Formula into practice in ways that create systemic and sustainable change. As you dive deep into this model, notice how we continue to stress the big idea that Leadership—whether it is self-leadership (individual level) or organizational leadership (organizational level)—is the Force Multiplier of everything good or bad.

Mastering the Reinvention Roadmap

The Reinvention Roadmap allows individuals and organizations to create a comprehensive Reinvention Game Plan (blueprint) that they can then execute against. It is a powerful framework because of its systemic and holistic nature. It captures all of the elements that need to be designed and aligned within an individual or organizational context in order for performance to be improved both now and in the future. It helps the individual or organizational architect easily see cause-and-effect relationships and to design for optimum results.

To understand the Reinvention Roadmap better, put yourself in the role of a newly promoted senior vice president of a new division within a Fortune 500 company.

Imagine you've been empowered by your CEO to build a new division from the ground up. She has given you all the resources needed to make it happen.

As background, your company has tried for three years to enter a particular market and establish a solid market position, but has failed every year. Your CEO is determined to create an entirely new division to focus on achieving success, with hopes of having a greater laser focus on achieving the outcome.

Before you officially launch the organization by hiring people, creating a strategy, and establishing processes, your CEO-mentor suggests that you spend three days alone at one of your favorite retreats, and, with flip chart pages and whiteboard at hand, create a master blueprint of the new organization. What should it look like? How should it be designed? She challenges you to "perfectly design the new division for world-class results and a number-one position in the marketplace within three years." She then asks you to come back to corporate and pitch it to her and her executive team. They are fully behind you.

THE REINVENTION ROADMAP™

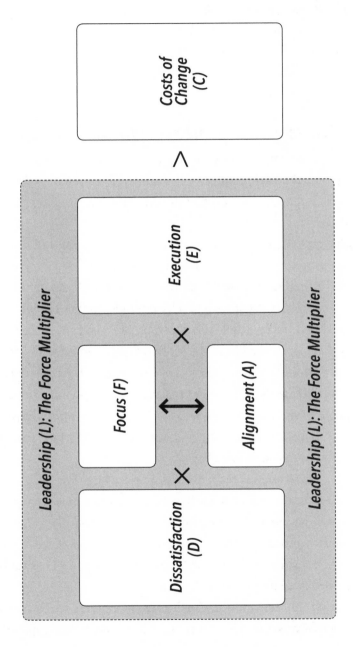

As one last recommendation, she asks you to use the Reinvention Roadmap to build your blueprint. To ensure that you have a deep and solid understanding of the Reinvention Roadmap model, your CEO tells you to use the Roadmap as if you were going through a seven-part story.

The Reinvention Roadmap at Work: Amazon in India

To get our arms around the Reinvention Roadmap as an implementation template and to better see the Reinvention Roadmap at work, let's take a look at Amazon.com's attempt to enter the market in India.

Jeff Bezos and Amazon.com have decided to go all-out in introducing ecommerce throughout all of India. To do this, Amazon recognizes they will need to completely reinvent how typical Indians—especially those with lower incomes—purchase goods. Indian cultural assumptions about buyer–seller relationships are radically different from those Amazon is used to in the United States and most Western parts of the world. In addition, there are extraordinary hurdles, such as the lack of credit cards (only fourteen percent of the population has them), ineffective banking processes, cash-only systems, an underwhelming infrastructure for cross-country commerce—mostly dirt roadways and poor communication systems.

But Bezos and his team are visionaries. They see India as the last great e-frontier on earth, with over one billion potential customers and a retail opportunity measured in the trillion-dollar range. Maybe even more important, Bezos is holding firm to one of the messages of Mavericks explained in our first chapter, The Age of Disruption: it is much better to disrupt than to be disrupted.

Using the Reinvention Equation as a template we can fill in each variable for this example to form the Reinvention Roadmap. With all of the elements clarified within the Reinvention Roadmap, we can get a sense of how well Amazon is doing at reinventing the way India conducts retail commerce.

- **Dissatisfaction:** On Amazon's side, they are still feeling embarrassed about their current performance in China, which is at just one percent of ecommerce. They admit to a severe lack of initial investment and now are paying for that shortage with slow growth. They will not let this happen in India, with such high stakes. On India's side, only ten percent of its citizens have access to modern retail, and the poor find it hard to get the essentials at a fair price.

- **Focus:** Within one warehouse found on the outskirts of Mumbai, Amazon's mission statement for the Indian business is hung on the wall: "Transforming how India sells, transforming how India buys." Bezos and his team have made it very clear that they expect India to eventually—and quickly—overtake Japan, Germany, and the United Kingdom as their largest overseas market. Amazon's focus is to be *the disrupter that completely reshapes commerce within India.*

- **Alignment:** Completely scrapping the traditional blocking and tackling infrastructure that they have used in other markets, Amazon seems to have landed on a model that works. Indian customers can visit a small storefront somewhere in the city staffed by a single person and containing a single laptop. An employee helps the customer place an order online. Amazon currently has four thousand small distribution centers scattered throughout India. Employees use motorcycles to get around and stuff their backpacks full of deliveries. Delivery points are not homes but small shops whose owners have volunteered as pick-up locations. Amazon is currently using a cash-on-delivery model to get around the lack of credit cards.

- **Execution:** The culture of execution, as defined by the behaviors of Amazon leaders and workers, seems to center around five cultural priorities: speed, simplicity, flexibility, adaptability, and a win–win attitude. Everything happens at warp speed but is done as simply as possible. Constant learning and adaptability is at a premium, and ensuring that the small shop owners acting as delivery points know exactly what's in it for them is the best kind of win–win.

- **Leadership:** Amazon India is led by Amit Agarwal, a Mumbai native and Stanford University graduate who embodies the local culture and is empowered to reinvent Amazon's business model. Agarwal worked right next to Bezos over the past sixteen years and also embodies everything about Amazon. Agarwal is the true force multiplier behind Amazon's success, along with the other leaders he has chosen and trained. They are piecing together an immensely complex puzzle, building everything from scratch, and doing so much of it through their trusting relationships with the people of India.

- **Cost of Change:** The cost barriers of successful entry and formation of a new business model in India—along with the challenge of working against the common retail assumptions of most of the world—is huge. Making the costs even larger is Amazon's inability to follow their number-one business model practice: to buy products in huge bulk at wholesale prices. Each of India's twenty-nine states has a different tax code, making cross-country shipping laborious, not to mention the challenging national infrastructure—a decrepit manufacturing system, bad highways and railroads, very little high-speed connectivity, and limited banking services.

On the next page is an example of some of the choices Amazon India has made, fit within the Reinvention Roadmap, so you can see how they have striven for alignment among the elements.

The long-term results of Amazon's aggressive expansion into India still remain to be seen. But the key elements and choices Amazon had to make—Focus, Alignment, Execution, and Leadership—seem well suited for the task at hand, reinforced by their strong dissatisfaction for the poor performance in China. Success

EXAMPLE: THE REINVENTION ROADMAP™ FOR AMAZON IN INDIA

Leadership (L)
The Force Multiplier

Amit Agarwal was hand picked by Jeff Bezos to run Amazon India. The Mumbai native and Standford graduate is intimately familiar with both the formal and informal cultural idiosyncrasies of India, and has been totally empowered to reinvent Amazon's business model to match the reinvention of Indian commerce. He and the team he selected role model the attributes desired in all leaders.

Dissatisfaction (D)

India: Only 10% of Indians have access to modern retail, and most find it difficult getting basic goods for a fair price.

Amazon: Must rebound from poor performance in China and show they have the industrial know-how to scale globally and transform the way the world shops.

×

Focus (F)

- Amazon India Purpose Statement: "Transforming how India sells, transforming how India buys."
- To disrupt, and not be disrupted.

↔

Alignment (A)

- Small storefronts with laptop ordering stations (and someone to explain how)
- Small, local distribution centers with deliveries made by motorbikes
- Delivery points at local shops
- Cash-on-delivery model

×

Execution (E)

- Speed
- Simplicity
- Flexibility
- Win-win approach
- Adaptability

>

Costs of Change (C)

- New business model
- Building everything from scratch formally and informally
- Challenging national infrastructure
- 29 different tax codes

will depend on how well Amazon's Reinvention design overcomes the significant costs of change.

Seven Reinvention Roadmap Story Lines

The Reinvention Roadmap is a detailed and comprehensive translation of the Reinvention Formula. This framework is a working model that is used as an implementation template when engaging in Reinvention. The Reinvention Roadmap actually guides you through linear steps and helps you iterate your individual or organizational reinvention game plan until you have designed your organization to the optimal level.

To understand the Reinvention Roadmap better, think about it as comprising seven key story lines. Each of the story lines builds on the others until the masterpiece Reinvention Roadmap and game plan is created.

Story Line 1: Establishing Your Level of Dissatisfaction (D): Before launching a Reinvention and beginning to make critical design choices, it must be clear and transparent to everyone involved that change must happen. And that it must happen quickly and in quantum ways. The key question that is asked in the first story line is "Among leaders and employees, is the level of dissatisfaction with the status quo high enough that they will fully commit their time, emotions, and effort to the reinvention effort?" Unless the answer is a firm "yes," there will be no other story lines until the dissatisfaction is at the right level to proceed.

Story Line 2: Making Effective Focus and Alignment Design Choices (F x A): When trying to reinvent an organization for better results, the lead architect generally has twelve major design choices that he or she can influence.

The first four design choices are *Focus* design choices. They are strategic in nature and set high-level direction for everyone to work toward. The four choices are: 1) Vision and Mission; 2) Strategies and Differentiators; 3) Business Model; and 4) Goals and Measures.

The second six choices are *Alignment* design choices. They are more operational in nature. The purpose of Alignment design choices is to put the infrastructure in place to implement and operationalize the Focus design choices.

The final design choices encompass Execution and Leadership, and we will explain those in following story lines.

To ensure that the best choices are made in these initial ten categories, it is always good to conduct an environmental scan when you initially launch. This will confirm that the new organization is not designed in a vacuum, but will consider the needs of customers and stakeholders and will understand industry dynamics and trends.

Story Line 3: Ensuring Execution (Employee Behaviors) Will Drive Desired Results (E): Research again and again shows that the number one influencer of individual and organizational results is the culture, or typical behaviors, of the person or organization on a day-to-day basis. It is what people do, or don't do, that drives the results they get.

The most effective way to improve results is to simply readjust what people do on a daily basis. To do this is a matter of 1) identifying the desired behaviors that will drive the desired results; 2) ensuring that the Focus and Alignment design choices, working together, will encourage that behavior (employee behavior can always be better understood when you remind yourself that the behavior is most likely rational to the people exhibiting it and is usually driven by the ten design choices they've made); and 3) iterating behaviors and design choices over and over again to make sure they support one another.

Story Line 4: Designing a Leadership System and Culture that Force Multiplies Everything Good and Desired (L): It is leadership that activates and sets in motion all of the other eleven elements talked about above. It is leadership who influences the design and implementation and accountability for the elements. The Leadership System needs to clearly inform leaders of expected behaviors, attitudes, style, and overall cohesive culture and tone set.

Story Line 5: Ensuring the Draft Design Will Achieve the Desired Results: At the end of the day, individuals and organizations are in the business of getting great results. The saying, "no profit, no mission" is true. This step is similar to Story Line 3 in that you determine what the end-in-mind is (desired results), and then ask yourself the question "Will the design choices we made in the Reinvention Formula equation $(D \times F \times A \times E)$ L drive the desired results that we are targeting?" If not, then you and your team must continue to iterate the design until you are confident you have done your best at architecting a high-performance organization.

Story Line 6: Calculating the Cost of Change (C): The last step in the Reinvention Roadmap is calculating the cost of change. The key question asked here is "Will the twelve design choices, combined together, be strong and dynamic enough to overpower the cost of change?" In this step we simply quantify or qualify the cost of change and then answer the question. Without a firm "yes," the architect and team should return to the drawing board.

Story Line 7: Iterate the Reinvention Roadmap until It Is the Best Possible Design (C): The last step in the Reinvention Roadmap is the process of iterating the design until it is at its optimal level. The key question asked here is "Will the twelve design choices, combined together, be powerful enough to achieve the results that the organization is trying to achieve?" This step involves tweaking and refining until everyone in the room feels they have the best chance of success going forward.

Having taught you these seven compelling story lines, your CEO expresses her confidence that, with the help of the Reinvention Roadmap template, you will return with a successful blueprint for her and the executive team to review and refine.

Your confidence skyrockets as you realize that your three-day personal retreat will not be a shoot-from-the-hip exercise, but a well-thought-out process that leads you to the right choices. You also realize the importance of having a common language and framework that you can use with your new team as you work through the Roadmap.

Defining the Reinvention Sub-Elements

The following table lists the sub-elements that belong in each of the major areas of the Reinvention Roadmap.

REINVENTION ROADMAP
Sub-Element Definitions

(D) Dissatisfaction with the Status Quo	**Financial:** total revenues and profits–or total compensation and benefits.
	Morale: the attitude and feelings of either you or your employees.
	Health: physical, mental, emotional, and spiritual health that has been impacted by your profession and work atmosphere. General health of the company.
	Reputation: the perception that your peers have of you and your organization.
	Future: your confidence in the future health of your career and organization.
(F) Focus Design Choices	**Vision:** a description of the desired future state that is highly energizing.
	Mission: the true purpose, passion, and reason for existence.
	Strategies: key multiyear strategic actions will help achieve mission and vision.
	Differentiators: a clear description of what is unique and different from peers.
	Business Model: an easily understood model of how money will be made and the core value-add provided.
	Goals: the accomplishments to be made during the first year of reinvention.
	Measures: the key metrics that will ultimately determine winning and losing.

(Continued)

(A) Alignment Design Choices	**Processes and Tasks:** the daily repetitious processes and tasks needed to achieve the mission, vision, strategies, and goals.
	Structure and Relationships: the key relationships needed and the organization's structure, roles, and responsibilities.
	Information and Decisions: the information and knowledge needed on a weekly basis to make the best choices. The key decisions to be made on a weekly basis that promote success.
	People, Skills, and Rewards: the types of people in the organization, the skills they need, and how they are rewarded and recognized.
	Technology and Equipment: the simple technologies and equipment that must be in place in order to work efficiently.
	Paradigms and Values: ensuring that worldviews and mind-sets are based upon reality and enable success rather than inhibit it.
(E) Execution Design Choices (Behaviors)	**Proactive:** never reacting or playing the victim, but acting based upon dearly held values.
	Visionary: maintaining focus on the ultimate "end in mind" instead of getting bogged down in details and useless tasks.
	Accountable: always acting in accordance with values, and being accountable when deadlines are missed.
	Resilience: when rejected, turned away, or experiencing failure, eventually jumping up, dusting yourself off, and moving forward with fierce resolve.
	Win–win: operating each day with a win–win attitude and with an effort to make the pie larger for everyone.
	Innovative: constantly questioning the status quo and looking for ways to do things better, faster, and cheaper.
	Adaptive: using judo skills when handling incoming global shockwaves.
(L) Leadership Design Choices	**Make It Happen:** simply making great things happen on a consistent basis regardless of circumstance.
	Stamina, Resilience, and Forward Movement: leading even when it is tough, and constantly pushing toward the "vision" finish line. Always maintaining forward momentum.
	Create Willing Followers: leading in a way that creates willing followers.
	Vision and Execution: setting clear end-points and setting the stage for flawless execution to happen.
	Empowerment and Accountability: understanding that it is "the front line that produces the bottom-line" and setting clear boundaries and metrics for performance.
(C) Cost of Change	**Time:** the amount of discretionary time demanded during reinvention.
	Money: the possible loss of money during the transition from current state to desired state.
	Relationship: the potential loss of important relationships.
	Reputation: the potential dents to public and professional image.

Creating Your Reinvention Roadmap

Now you are ready to experience the tangible process of Reinvention!

There are eleven steps in creating either your individual or organizational Reinvention Roadmap. These steps don't necessarily follow the seven-part story line in every detail, but it will be clear as you work through the exercises why they are in the order that they are.

We recommend that you keep a visual copy of the Reinvention Roadmap by your side as you work through this 11-step process. A best practice is to create a large poster of the Reinvention Roadmap Framework and post it on a wall in the room you are using for your design work.

Below are summary explanations of each exercise. These are not intended to be the detailed directions for every step. These explanations are simply to help you understand the flow of the overall Reinvention Roadmap process.

Our website, www.ageofdisruption.com, contains detailed exercises, as well as templates for each step.

11 Reinvention Roadmap Exercises

1. Conduct an Environmental Scan

2. Create and Communicate a Case for Change

3. Define Future Desired Results with Clear Success Metrics

4. Craft Focus Design Choices

5. Construct Alignment Design Choices

6. Identify Desired Execution Behaviors

7. Identify Leadership Strategies and Style

8. Calculate the Cost of Change

9. Refine and Iterate Reinvention Roadmap

10. Capture and Communicate Lessons Learned

11. Determine Timeline for Next Reinvention Roadmap Exercise

Exercise 1: Conduct an Environmental Scan

- **Purpose:** To understand the demands and trends of the external environment. The external environment can include important constituents such as customers, peers, competition, industry, and other stakeholders.

- **Outcome:** A document that includes findings from each individual scan and a summary of themes, lessons learned, and implications. A newfound confidence that the organization is not being designed in a self-serving, internally focused vacuum.

Exercise 2: Create and Communicate a Case for Change (D)

- **Purpose:** To create a powerful case for change that clearly outlines in a quantitative and qualitative fashion why Reinvention must happen now. To spark passion in others to join forces with you and your team to make it happen.

- **Outcome:** A communication document or platform that explains in easily understood language why change is important to each individual, customer, and stakeholder. To answer the question for all individuals involved in the Reinvention, "What's in it for me?"

Exercise 3: Define Future Desired Results with Clear Success Metrics

- **Purpose:** To clearly state the desired outcomes that are expected to be achieved once Reinvention is accomplished. To ensure that there are metrics established that will enable the organization to track progress.

- **Outcome:** To give everyone that will be affected by the Reinvention a clear idea of what the expected and desired results are with the new organization, along with a clear idea of how the results will be measured.

Exercise 4: Craft Focus Design Choices (F)

- **Purpose:** To make new strategic design choices in the four elements within the Focus area of the Reinvention Roadmap.

- **Outcome:** To ensure that the new strategic choices around Mission and Vision, Strategies and Differentiators, Business Model, and Goals and Measures are exactly tailored to positively influence the external environment and become the market leader. To ensure that each person understands the role he or she will play in the future of the organization in terms of how his or her passion aligns with the organization's strategic passion and direction.

Exercise 5: Construct Alignment Design Choices (A)

- **Purpose:** To make new operational design choices in the six elements within the Alignment area of the Reinvention Roadmap.

- **Outcome:** To ensure that the new infrastructure choices are exactly what is needed to put the new organization's Focus elements into action. To ensure that all six design choice elements are aligned with one another in synergistic ways. To use this process to get feedback from the masses regarding what they feel are the best operational design choices for the new organization.

Exercise 6: Identify Desired Execution Behaviors (E)

- **Purpose:** To identify and list the behaviors that are required of leaders and employees in the new organization in order to achieve the new and accelerated results that are expected.

- **Outcome:** To use this process to get feedback and buy-in from leaders and employees on what they feel are best-in-class behaviors that all should emulate going forward. To break it down into specific and tangible behaviors so there is no mistaking what is expected. To begin designing all the HR and talent management elements that must be in place to support this.

Exercise 7: Identify Leadership Strategies and Style (L)

- **Purpose:** To identify the new leadership model needed, including leadership strategies, leadership style, best practices, and the criteria that will be used to select and train leaders.

- **Outcome:** To use this process to collect feedback and buy-in from leaders and potential leaders on what leadership strategies and models must be emulated going forward. To begin designing all the HR and talent management elements that must be in place to support this.

Exercise 8: Calculate the Cost of Change (C)

- **Purpose:** To quantify and qualify the true cost of change in a way that is clear and visible to all. To challenge leaders and employees to validate or refine the list.

- **Outcome:** To create a document that details all the potential costs of change and the power of each cost in terms of holding back implementation of the new design.

Exercise 9: Refine and Iterate Reinvention Roadmap (Until It Is "Perfectly Designed")

- **Purpose:** To step back after the initial design blueprint is in place and return to test its likelihood of achieving the expected desired results. To continue to refine and iterate until the design is the best it can be.

- **Outcome:** To give others a chance to understand the new design and provide feedback that would make it even stronger. To use this opportunity to get the buy-in of all those who will be affected by the new, reinvented organization.

Exercise 10: Capture and Communicate Lessons Learned

- **Purpose:** To cap off a great design effort by establishing a team to review the Reinvention Roadmap process and identify lessons learned.

- **Outcome:** To visibly show the behaviors of a learning organization and to capture new learnings that will help other organizations that attempt Reinvention.

Exercise 11: Determine Timeline for Next Reinvention Roadmap Exercise

- **Purpose:** To make sure that the Reinvention Roadmap exercise will be repeated in the future.

- **Outcome:** To show customers, employees, and stakeholders that there is a commitment to ongoing performance excellence.

COMPLIMENTARY TOOLS AND TEMPLATES FOR REINVENTION ROADMAP

For complimentary access to comprehensive instructions, templates, and tools for the eleven Reinvention Roadmap exercises, please visit our website at www.ageofdisruption.com. You can download these for your individual or organizational use.

The Reinvention Roadmap in Action: The Case of the BYU Football Team

We have been actively watching this case study unfold for many years. The head coach of the BYU football team, Bronco Mendenhall, has used Reinvention principles to turn around a losing football team to become one that is greatly admired.

This case helps to illustrate the different design choices made in the Reinvention Roadmap framework, and the importance of overall alignment.

Presenting Situation

The nationally respected Brigham Young University football team was at a crossroads in 2004.

BYU had won the NCAA football championship in 1984 under legendary coach LaVell Edwards. But the school's proud tradition of winning was evaporating, as was the squeaky-clean image of the private, Christian church–owned school. Not only was the team coming off back-to-back losing seasons, but there was also a significant increase in off-field incidents that were both highly public and unacceptable.

Change had to be made, and the public was demanding that it happen quickly. Dissatisfaction (D) was squarely in place.

BYU Football's Design Choice Architect

BYU promoted the team's defensive coordinator, Bronco Mendenhall, to be the new head coach. Although he had no prior experience as a head coach, he was well liked by players for being direct, honest, hardworking, and committed to core values. This was a guy who BYU's leaders believed could bring the team into compliance with the school's core values and also win.

One of our colleagues taught Mendenhall that a key role he needed to fill was that of organizational architect. As the architect and designer of the football team's destiny, he used a framework that helped him make intentional design choices that would transform the losing football team into one that not only won games but also complied with the school's honor code.

Over the next few years, Coach Bronco, by combining the best of college football 101 with the best of organizational reinvention, pulled off a remarkable reinvention.

Bold and Courageous Design Choices

Mendenhall included others in the reinvention process. And he taught them that they all needed to begin by creating a compelling focus. Then it would be time to align the processes, systems, and structures of the football program to achieve their new vision. Bronco and the team made courageous and innovative design choices during their first few years. Note below how the design choices support one another in the Reinvention Formula framework.

Reinvention Element	Design Choices
Focus	**Mission**: Mendenhall and his staff made the team's mission "to be the flag bearer of the school." According to Mendenhall, "It became clear to me that I was to make the football program as distinct as possible because the university's purpose is so distinct and unique. Spirit is what we represent." **Strategic Differentiator**: Mendenhall strongly believed that BYU's stringent honor code could be used to the program's advantage and made no apologies for the way he expected his players to conduct themselves both in public and in private. **Goals**: football was listed as #5, behind faith, family, knowledge, and friends, on a list of priorities that Mendenhall gives his players and anyone else who will listen.
Alignment	**Work Processes**: Mendenhall noted that when he took over as head coach, he realized that the offense and defense were on totally separate pages. So he created strength-conditioning teams blended from both sides to build one culture. And practices were restructured as highly disciplined events. **Structure and People**: Mendenhall realized right away that building the talent on his football team depended on finding recruits who not only could play Division I football, but also were prepared for the spiritual and academic rigors of BYU's environment. According to Mendenhall, "We call the bishop, stake president, minister, pastor, rabbi–whoever is in charge of the young man's spiritual growth–and ask them, 'Can this young man thrive in this environment?' If they don't answer in the affirmative, we move on." **Decision Making**: the coaches began building strong ties with former BYU football players from all over the United States and across the world, asking them to act as the team's eyes and ears identifying potential players for the program. **Information**: Mendenhall used a strategy called "visual management" to disseminate important information and values. All walls have pictures, mementos, or symbols of what is most important to the program, both past and present.

(Continued)

Reinvention Element	Design Choices
Execution	**Traditions**: Mendenhall is a fan of symbolism and used a lot of it to show his young men the culture he wanted them to model.
	Fall Camp: on the eve of Mendenhall's first fall camp as head coach, the roar of 65,000 fans echoed across the empty stands of LaVell Edwards Football Stadium. Scattered across the football field, 105 football players lay on their backs in street clothes, eyes closed, as voices from the past projected from the loudspeakers and told of the famous plays from BYU's storied past.
	Spring Camp: on the night before the first spring game, Mendenhall, without warning, had his players and coaches board a bus. They headed up Provo Canyon, where a bonfire was awaiting them. Mendenhall had each of his team leaders take a group of players. Handing out paper and pens, Mendenhall had all the players write down everything that was wrong with the football team. Then each player read his paper and threw it into the bonfire. Finally, when all the pages had turned to ashes, Mendenhall held up one of the helmets the team had used during their losing season. He said, "We are not going to look like this anymore." And then, for good measure, he threw the baseball cap he had worn as the defensive coordinator and proclaimed, "And we're not gong to play like this anymore."
	Worldview: every player was given a plain gray T-shirt with the words "Band of Brothers" printed on it. They all wore these T-shirts, including the coaches, during games to promote teamwork.
	Feelings: before every Saturday game during the season, no matter where the game was in the country, the BYU football team held Friday night firesides at local LDS meetinghouses. Everyone in the community was invited to attend. These gatherings had the coaches and players speak and sing.
Leadership	**Creating Willing Followers**: during his first season, Mendenhall told his team that they were going to have a "race to the Y"–a large white Y painted on the mountainside above BYU's campus. To get to the Y is a rigorous one-and-a-half-mile climb. Mendenhall participated in the race, reaching the top before his players, and was the first to congratulate them on their accomplishment. After this, the team was ready to do anything for their new coach.
	Shared Leadership: Mendenhall instituted a players' leadership council, made up of elected representatives of each position on the football team. Through the council, players could voice ideas and concerns to the coaches.

Cougar Reinvention Results

The reinvention of BYU football under Bronco Mendenhall has been an incredible success. His results over the last eleven years speak for themselves:

99 Wins	69.7% Winning
43 Losses	

- 11 straight bowl invitations
- Record of 99–43
- BYU signed a nine-year contract with ESPN for at least six games a year on national television
- Strong team identity with stakeholders
- Visible flag bearers of the university

Whether you are leading a college football team yourself or leading a company, the elements of the Reinvention Formula are universal. The BYU case demonstrates the importance of strong leadership and the impact leaders can have when they view their organization from the perspective of an organizational architect.

As a footnote, Bronco agreed after the 2015 season to be the new head football coach at the University of Virginia. In his first press conference, he laid out his strategy for turning the 4–8 UVA football team around, and it followed the same principles found in the Reinvention Formula and Roadmap that he used successfully at BYU. Bronco's goal? To boost and accelerate results through disruptive and proactive change.

Apple Perfection Executed Flawlessly

When did you have your best-ever shopping experience? Whom were you purchasing from, and what made it special? Did you gush about this experience to friends?

We love Apple products. But as great as we feel about the products, it is the store experience that really creates deep loyalty, despite premium prices.

A few months ago, we needed to buy a power cord for our Mac-Book Pro. We walked into our local Apple store, and the first thing we noticed was that the "yellow" shirt people (Apple employees) actually outnumbered the customers.

Two employees, situated to meet us as soon as we walked in, greeted us and asked how they could help. We told them what we needed, and one said, "Follow me."

Expert Insight: Luciano Pezzotta

The chapter starts with a compelling story of a home-building firm that learned the powerful principle that organizations are "perfectly designed" to get the results that they get. And this principle seems true with individuals too.

I'm impressed with how clear this chapter reinforces this organizing principle. This is a powerful setup regarding the need for a systemic and processes-oriented framework like the Reinvention Roadmap to guide those courageous souls willing to launch a reinvention effort. The seven story lines are a great way to summarize the Reinvention Roadmap and how it will truly allow people and companies to handle the craziness of the Age of Disruption.

The Brigham Young University football team is a great wrap-up in showing how all of the choices within the Reinvention Roadmap must be aligned and well-thought-out.

Key Insights

I found the following insights most powerful for me.

Reinvention Must Originate from Deep within the Heart, Mind, and Soul
Reinvention requires a holistic effort. It requires connecting strategy to the external environmental demands, then aligning processes, systems, and structure to the strategy to ensure it can be executed. But the most important element is culture. That is true individually and organizationally. Culture is the heart, mind, and soul behind great results. It is what will drive change and cause it to stick.

Reinvention Is Not Free
Because reinvention can be launched as a strategic corporate effort, the cost of execution is often overlooked. It seems that organizations can be caught unaware by unexpected costs in the middle of their reinvention journey. This can be true on intangible things like reputation, relationships, morale, and other things. If this happens, employees and leaders often begin questioning the original rationale for the reinvention, and this creates a self-fulfilling prophecy.

Investing in Change Management Is Key
Resistance to change shouldn't be shocking to any of us. We love our comfort zones and actually spend energy protecting them. Organizations (and we as individuals) should recognize that there is almost a 100-percent chance it will happen. So prepare for it. Education, involvement, and two-way communication are crucial.

Effort and Results Are Not Linear
Let's face it. Sometimes it takes time to produce impressive results when you reinvent. Sticking to your commitments is critical. Just like when you are trying to become more healthy and lose weight, you sometimes do not see immediate results after you leave the gym. Keep in mind the vision of a new you and the benefits you were hoping to attain when you originally launched your effort.

Systems Thinking Is a Must

Organizations are a house of cards. Make your choices wisely, and recognize the impact on other previous design choices.

Application to My Career

Coming from an analytical and academic background and possessing a hyper-rational personality, planning was never an issue for me. Many times, however, things turned out different from my plan. It took perseverance to come out the other side successful. No individual or organizational reinvention is possible without that extra sense of urgency and energy that gets you out of bed each morning with the attitude of making it happen. Having ample dissatisfaction and a powerful vision in place to motivate 24/7 is critical.

In my career, I have had to reinvent myself multiple times. And it is not easy. One time, it was transforming myself from an investment banker into a management consultant. Another time, it involved a career move to Asia from my home country and adopting an entirely new culture. I can never forget the times when I launched new businesses with very little corporate support. Each reinvention, no doubt, requires us to humbly yet boldly confront the brutal facts and deeply question how we think, work, collaborate, and even talk.

Advice to the Reader

The Reinvention Roadmap is a tool that you will want to frame on your office wall, save in your Dropbox folders, be able to pull up on your smartphone, and keep at an arm's length. The systemic and powerful tool has the width, depth, and wisdom to guide you should you choose to reinvent either individually or personally. The Reinvention Roadmap will challenge you with the right questions and provide you the right process to do the right things. Then it is just a matter of doing them right!

As a leader of an organization that has a choice to fade into irrelevance or reinvent, before you lies a challenging path that will require your utmost dedication to vision, energy, resilience, and execution. You can either flee or fight. If you choose to fight, give yourself the best possible chance at success, and use the right strategies, processes, and tools as you reinvent.

About the Expert

Luciano Pezzotta is the founder and managing partner of the European Center for Strategic Innovation, a global research and executive-education firm focused on strategy and innovation. He is also a corporate advisor, experienced entrepreneur, and a master Blue Ocean Strategy practitioner.

He has founded multiple ventures in various sectors, including Digitaltech International, a high-tech firm that specializes in disruptive telematics solutions, and the Blue Ocean Garden Beach Resort, in Thailand. Pezzotta is an adjunct faculty member at the Singapore Institute of Management and holds a masters of science in international management from Bocconi University.

Chapter Six

◇◇

REINVENTION ACCELERATORS

TOOLS TO ENABLE AND
ENHANCE FLAWLESS REINVENTION

*"Never give up, for that is just the place and time
when the tide will turn."*

—*Harriet Beecher Stowe*

Ambush in Afghanistan

In 2005, four Navy SEALs were inserted into the Hindu Kush region of Afghanistan. Taliban leader Ahmad Shah had recently killed more than twenty US Marines, as well as villagers and refugees who were aiding American forces. The four-man SEAL Team 10, part of Operation Red Wings, was charged with tracking down and killing Shah.

After being discovered by three Taliban sheepherders, the team leader aborted the mission. As the Navy SEAL team members began their hike out of the region, they were soon surrounded by more than 50 armed Taliban fighters located above them on a rugged mountain. All four men took their positions, and the battle began.

In the end, three of the four Navy SEALs were killed. Despite being outnumbered by nine to one, being far downhill from the enemy, and facing an avalanche of AK-47 fire, rocket-propelled grenades, and 82mm mortars, the fight lasted almost three hours. The

SEALs killed almost half of the insurgents (twenty-three) before the fight ended. Marcus Luttrell was the lone survivor.

The Exponential Power of Accelerators

Navy SEALs are among the toughest fighters on the planet. But for a four-person Navy SEAL team to inflict this much damage when facing such overwhelming odds is incredible. How did they do it?

The answer lies in three powerful enablers, or accelerators, the armed forces reinforces in each Navy SEAL throughout his career. In the case of Operation Red Wings, these accelerators allowed the four-person team to fight as if they were a much larger and more powerful force.

1. **Mind-set:** A Navy SEAL's mental toughness might even be more important than his physical strength. The Navy has found four mental factors that are the most critical in helping a SEAL be successful in live combat situations:

    a. **Goal setting:** SEALs need to constantly have short-term goals ("I can make it through one more minute"); midterm goals ("I can make it to the end of the week"); and long-term goals ("I want to be a Navy SEAL").

    b. **Mental rehearsal:** The Navy SEAL always sees himself succeeding in future assignments.

    c. **Self-talk:** The average person says between three hundred and seven thousand words to themselves per minute. If the majority of this self-talk is negative, a SEAL will definitely fail. They are trained to engage in realistic self-talk.

    d. **Arousal control:** The ability to think clearly during a stressful situation is lessened when a SEAL becomes scared, anxious, or worried. The brain is flooded with chemicals that make it almost impossible to make fast and accurate decisions. SEALs are taught breathing techniques to control blood flow to the head.

2. **Training and conditioning:** Recruits are required to go through eighteen months of full-time training before they can be recognized as Navy SEALs. During this time they receive the following education: leadership skills, mental stamina, physical stamina, combat diving, land warfare, teamwork, parachuting, advanced weapons, land navigation, close-quarters combat, medical skills, resistance, survival, demolition, and escape training.

3. **Equipment and gear:** A SEAL always has on him equipment and gear that will allow him to operate in any situation. The core items are headgear, a tactical vest, sunglasses, an escape and evasion kit, a KA-BAR knife, a weapon and scope, a tactical backpack, lightweight boots, food, water, and tactical gloves.

Whether you are reinventing yourself or leading your organization through quantum change, you will also need to equip yourself with the right accelerating strategies and tools to significantly increase the probability of success and the acceleration of results that you desire.

Five Reinvention Accelerators

Our consulting experience suggests five Reinvention Accelerators that have proven to be highly effective for our clients to make significant change happen and stick over the long-term.

Accelerator 1: Adopting Effective Leader Sets: Ensuring that you and your organization adopt mind-sets, skill sets, tool sets, and behavioral sets in ways that enable you to get superior results.

Accelerator 2: Leveraging Whole-Brain Thinking: Ensuring that all four human brain preferences are tapped into, and leveraged, when designing and implementing reinvention.

Accelerator 3: Crafting a Powerful Leadership Brand: Ensuring you use the reinvention exercise to craft a powerful leadership brand for you or the organization you are leading.

Accelerator 4: Being a Reinvention Champion: Ensuring accountability and implementation of ten powerful attributes of successful Reinvention Champions.

Accelerator 5: Preserving Work–Life Balance: Ensuring an all-out effort to be as balanced as possible when undergoing the fast and quantum change reinvention expects.

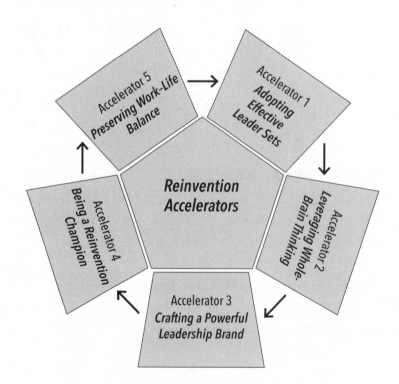

Accelerator 1: Adopting Effective Leader Sets

Our experience in personal and organizational change suggests that it takes a full commitment to enhancing a person or organization's *Leader Sets* to ultimately be effective.

We've coined the term Leader Sets as a way of grouping four critical components that must be constantly refined and ultimately aligned for "boots-on-the-ground" change to happen.

These four components are: Mind-sets, Skill sets, Tool sets, and Behavioral sets.

LEADER-SETS PROCESS

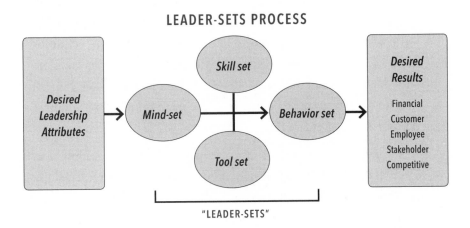

When interpreting the Leader-Sets Framework, it is best to start from left to right. The following three story lines seem to help with understanding how these four sets are organized.

1. **Mind-Sets:** We cannot state strongly enough how much mind-sets influence the other three sets. Significant change will not happen in the other three sets without an appropriate mind-set shift.

    Mind-sets are how we see and think about the world. Each of us views life through unique lenses based upon our background and powerful experiences such as education, childhood, culture, economic class, traumatic life events, religion, health issues, and so forth. These have all combined to shape our unique worldview.

We often tell clients that if you want to know why certain people within their organization are doing what they are doing, it is important to try to understand their fundamental mind-set as a person. This will help you connect the dots.

It is outdated, distorted, and unhelpful mind-sets that need to be rebooted and reprogrammed, just like a computer's foundational operating system, in order for reinvention to have a chance. Is not a new feeling of dissatisfaction simply a mind-set change? So the first set that must change is mind-set.

2. **Skill Sets and Tool Sets:** In the 21st century, human capital will be the ultimate competitive advantage. Having the right skills and tools will be crucial in the knowledge economy. Technologies, equipment, and other infrastructure are simply enablers for leaders and employees to use to implement their chosen strategy. These must be put in place after mind-sets are better aligned to current reality.

   a. *Skill sets* represent the knowledge, skills, and capabilities that each of us has developed over the years. We learn these through education, mentoring, reading, watching, and doing. If employees are too passive, they will wake up one day to find that their skill sets are hopelessly outdated. Our experience suggests that gaining new skill sets is a far easier task than shifting an outdated and ineffective mind-set.

   b. *Tool sets* are technologies, equipment, and templates that are used to help get tasks done more effectively and efficiently. Included in this category are computers and the software and templates that make them useful; handheld devices and apps; and facilities and equipment that enable greater productivity.

3. **Behavioral Sets:** Once mind-sets have been shifted to a better place and are aligned to a more genuine reality, and we have incorporated the necessary skills and tools into our daily work, it is now time to implement these through actions. Behavioral sets are behaving in ways that enable you to get better results. Behaviors are actual activities that you can see people visibly do.

Have you ever wondered why Walmart has essentially put Kmart into Chapter 11? Walmart decided to go head-to-head with Kmart in the big cities where Kmart was traditionally located. New customers began noticing that Walmart employees exhibited vastly superior behaviors than Kmart employees.

We conducted in-store benchmarking just to make sure our theory about Walmart versus Kmart was correct. Here is what we observed in just a short thirty-minute visit to each store:

1. **Greeting:** At Walmart we were greeted by a friendly war veteran in a wheelchair whose "Have a great day" felt genuine. At Kmart we experienced no greeting.

2. **Pointing:** When wandering around Kmart looking for the sporting goods section, we approached an employee in the women's department and asked for directions. She pivoted without moving, pointed to the back of the store, and said, "I think it is over in the back that way." We asked if she would take us there so that we didn't waste any more time (because she also didn't seem convinced she was right), and she answered, "I can't. I have to stay in my area." At Walmart the response to such a question is usually, "Follow me."

3. **Stocking shelves:** During our store visits we noticed that most Kmart employees were busy stocking the shelves, while Walmart employees seemed more approachable because we didn't feel we were interrupting their duties.

4. **Check-out:** During our Kmart visit we picked up some items for a family camping trip. Upon arriving at the checkout area we noticed a dozen checkout stations, but only one seemed to be open. We got in the back of a long line. When we finally were the next person in line, we noticed an employee sitting quietly at the register to our right. We asked, "Is this checkout line open?" She replied, "Yes."

   In contrast, as we approached the checkout area during our Walmart visit, a Walmart checkout person walked out to the main aisle, waved her hand above her head, and announced, "I am open on station fourteen."

Our benchmarking trip happened in 2014, almost thirty years after Kmart realized Walmart was a legitimate threat. Kmart employees' "boots-on-the-ground" behaviors haven't changed much in almost three decades. And it is employee behaviors that seem to be the biggest driver of results.

Refining Your Leader Sets

It can be helpful to begin identifying the mind-sets, skill sets, tool sets, and behavioral sets that must be in place in order to make successful reinvention happen. The four exercises below, with templates, can help you do this.

Exercise 1: Reframing Distorted Mind-Sets
The key word here is *reframing*. Distorted mind-sets often need not be completely erased but simply shifted two or three notches in either direction. It is a matter of reframing.

To complete the following exercise, please select up to two personal mind-sets that may be keeping you from making positive change. Use the grid to develop strategies that will help reframe those mind-sets to a better place.

a. Identify a distorted mind-set that might keep you from your true potential.	b. Identify the root cause that explains why you see the world with this mind-set.	c. Identify strategies that you could employ to reframe your mind-set to one that better aligns to reality.
Example Trying to change rarely works out for people.	**Example** Several years ago, the company I worked for announced a massive restructure. I knew it would not work out for me despite what my manager said. And I was right.	**Example** I'll read the book *Who Moved My Cheese?* to become more familiar with strategies to help me not only handle change but also leverage change to my benefit.

Exercise 2: Building New Skill Sets

Adopting and learning new skills involves investing time and effort into mastering a new competency. Sometimes that means doing this during discretionary time. To complete the following exercise, please select up to two of your skill sets that seem outdated. Use the following grid to identify strategies to improve those skill sets.

a. Identify a skill set that might be outdated, underutilized, or deficient in some way.	b. Identify possible reasons that this skill set needs attention.	c. Identify strategies that could help you bring this skill set to a higher level.
Example My personal planning skills are outdated.	Example I am a tactical person and love the feeling of making big task lists and knocking the tasks off.	Example I will check with our training department to see if there are any courses I can enroll in to help me be a more effective planner.

Exercise 3: Acquiring New Tool Sets

Tool sets are becoming more important in the 21st century. The Age of Disruption requires mastery of the latest technologies and templates. To complete the following exercise, please select up to two tool sets that you need to acquire if you are going to reach your potential through reinvention. Use the following grid to identify strategies to acquire these tool sets.

a. Identify a tool set that could help you increase your effectiveness and ability to reinvent yourself.	b. Identify reasons that you haven't adopted this necessary tool set yet.	c. Identify your plan for acquiring this tool set and your ability to use it effectively.
Example LinkedIn would help me stay current with important others.	Example I don't think I'm genetically wired to be a techie. I feel that technology is more work than it's worth. Why not just use a yellow legal pad and a pen and a phone to keep in touch with others?	Example My sister is an expert at LinkedIn. I will ask her if I can sign up for lessons.

Exercise 4: Implementing Effective Behavioral Sets

A person's behavior and/or an organization's culture is the most powerful driver of results. To complete the following exercise, please select up to two behavioral sets you most likely need to either adopt or upgrade. Use the grid to develop strategies to accomplish the upgrade.

a. Identify a behavioral set that you must upgrade or acquire for reinvention to be a success.	b. Identify why your current behavioral set is driving the wrong results.	c. Identify your plan to acquire this behavioral set as quickly and effectively as possible.
Example I should network with others internally and externally to my current organization.	**Example** I am naturally shy and tend to keep to myself rather than reach out to others.	**Example** I am going to join a few networking groups that will put me in situations where I will have to talk to others in my field.

The Power of Mind-Sets

Have you ever noticed that, when your mind-set and paradigms are distorted and not aligned to current reality, it is virtually impossible to make breakthrough change happen? This is true with organizational mind-sets as well. Many of the blindfolds we discussed in Chapter Two have distorted mind-sets as their true root cause. People and organizations simply become blind to reality.

Fareed Zakaria, a widely quoted CNN correspondent, recently said this about the West's inability to understand Vladimir Putin and what motivates and drives him:

> "Remember, Putin joined the KGB, Russia's spy service, in 1975, at the height of the Cold War, and he stayed in it until 1991. Literally when the Soviet Union collapsed is when he resigned from the KGB. Obama, in 1975, was playing basketball in Hawaii. These are very different people with a very different outlook on the world."

Zakaria was stating an important point about mind-sets. In order for the West to better understand Putin's actions, it needs to first understand his mind-set, his belief system, and his worldview. It is true that when you elect a president, you by default elect his or her mind-set as well. The behavior and decisions that we see from our president should be of no surprise.

We suggest that mind-sets are the ultimate driver behind individual and organizational behavior.

Stephen R. Covey once said that the only way to achieve a breakthrough is if you "break with" old ways of thinking. Columbus would have never dared cross the Atlantic thinking the world was flat. So what worldviews are you willing to *break with* in order to achieve remarkable break*throughs*?

Accelerator 2: Leveraging Whole-Brain Thinking

Have you ever wondered why you do and say the things you do? Better yet, have you ever wondered why others do and say the things they do? Understanding the *why* behind one another's behavior can help individuals and organizations work better with others when reinventing and can create cultures that benefit from the power of diversity.

Research shows that our brain is the source for why we think the way we think, say the things we say, and do the things we do. Our personalities and unique thinking and communicating styles don't originate from our bicep muscles or even our heart. They originate from our brain. This is the organ that makes us distinct and unique.

Discoveries of the Brain

The first big discovery regarding the brain occurred in the 1950s, when Dr. Roger Sperry found that the left half of the brain had different functions than the right half of the brain. Research conducted in the 1980s discovered that in addition to the top half of the brain, or cerebellum, there was also a bottom half, called the limbic system.

Ned Herrmann—the Father of Whole-Brain Thinking

Taking these two discoveries into account, Ned Herrmann, the manager of GE's Crotonville Training Facility at that time, began developing new ideas about *whole-brain thinking*.

He noted that there seemed to be four general thinking styles, and that they could be related to the four quadrants of the brain (upper left, lower left, upper right, lower right). Herrmann began using the strategy of whole-brain thinking to create leadership and management courses for GE leaders tailored to all four distinct thinking preferences.

Herrmann's research suggests that, while each of us can access all four quadrants of our brain, there are some quadrants we are more comfortable with than others. When we teach this concept to our clients, we have them write their name in cursive using their less preferred hand. We then ask them what it was like, and they usually respond with words like *uncomfortable, forced, hard*, and *awkward*.

Ned created a four-box framework called *The Whole Brain Model* to help people visualize the four different thinking styles of the brain. Today Herrmann International has the trademark on this powerful model.

Quadrant A	Quadrant D
Logical	Holistic
Analytical	Intuitive
Fact-Based	Integrating
Quantitative	Synthesizing
Quadrant B	**Quadrant C**
Organized	Interpersonal
Sequential	Feeling-Based
Planned	Kinesthetic
Detailed	Emotional

Whole-Brain Thinking Can Enable Successful Reinvention
So what's the strategy for optimizing whole-brain thinking? It is first to clearly understand your own brain profile, then try to understand others' brain profiles, and finally seek to communicate in ways that the listener can best understand.

To successfully reinvent either individually or organizationally, it is important to tap into all four quadrants.

For this book, we have created what we call the Whole Brain Reinventor Model. Each quadrant has questions you might ask during your reinvention to ensure that you are leveraging all four quadrant strengths of the brain.

Analyze	Strategize
• Do I know the expected ROI of this effort? • Does my plan seem logical and defensible? • Have I done an analysis of the issues that might keep me from successfully reinventing?	• Are my focus elements going to satisfy customers and stakeholders? • Do my focus elements clearly show my competitive advantage? • Do my focus elements reflect a deep understanding of the external environment? • Have I put together a balanced scorecard that can track my progress?
Organize	**Personalize**
• Do I have a comprehensive project plan? • Am I using an organized approach rather than just shooting from the hip? • Do I update my project plan based upon new information?	• Have I articulated the desired culture in a way that others can "see it"? • Have I looked at other high performers to see what best practices they have? • Have I taken into consideration the critical social networks that need to be in place?

Individual and Organizational Strategies

Here are a few practical strategies that will help you or your organization reinvent leveraging whole-brain thinking.

- **Individual Reinvention:** We suggest you invite a respected other to be your "reinvention coach." Some of us are "blind" in a few quadrants, and this coach can help you fill those gaps. Select a reinvention coach who has a slightly different HBDI (Herrmann Brain Dominance Instrument) profile than yours. Ask your coach to meet with you periodically to evaluate how you are doing in addressing the four quadrants.

- **Organizational Reinvention:** When conducting an organizational reinvention, it is always good to create a steering committee of people who together encompass a whole-brain perspective to oversee the reinvention. Nothing hinders a reinvention more than a team (steering committee and design) that views it from just one of the quadrants (making everything a Quadrant A financial decision).

The Talmud provides wise advice when it comes to thinking and working with others in a whole-brain way:

We do not see things as they are.
We see things as we are.

Accelerator 3: Crafting a Powerful Leadership Brand

When you are at work, and you walk into a room full of people who know you well, what opinion do they have of you as a professional? Do they see you as innovative? How about someone who just "gets things done"? Whether we are leaders or employees, we show up every day to work. The question is *"How do you want to show up?"*

A leadership brand is simply defined as "what you are primarily known for as a leader." It answers the question, "If you could write down just one sentence that best describes Sally as a leader, what would it be?" Your personal leadership brand, and your organization's leadership brand, is a high-value intangible that enables others to self-select whether they want to engage with you or not.

One glance at the following leadership examples makes it clear which brand messages they emote.

Leader	Charles Barkley	Angela Merkel	Tim Cook	Taylor Swift
	• Opinionated	• Bold	• Courageous	• Nice
	• Brash	• Consensus	• Fair	• Confident
	• Funny	• Proud	• Operational	• Leader
	• Basketball	• German	• Complimentary	• Millennial
Organization	Toyota	Nike	Google	Wegmans
	• Durable	• Innovative	• Fun	• Family
	• Quality	• Competitive	• Disruptive	• Expansive
	• Value	• Athletes	• Young	• Premium
	• Japan	• Swoosh	• Silicon Valley	• Friendly

Points of Differentiation

Note that every individual and organization found in the grid above isn't wildly popular with everyone. They each have their loyal following and also their noisy detractors. Great leader and organizational brands are laser focused and narrow. They adhere to the critical Michael Porter principle of "differentiation" and never attempt to be all things to all people.

We all want to show up in valuable ways in our professional and organizational sphere of influence. How do you ultimately want to show up? What clear and differentiated brand do you want to be known for?

Leadership Brand Framework

The following *Leadership Brand Framework* is a simple way to look at the components of a powerful leadership brand and how those components relate to one another. We believe that professional effectiveness begins with high character and high competence. These are the building blocks that leaders in the 21st century must master if they are to be effective with others over time.

- **Character** is at the core of who we are as individuals. It is composed of attributes such as integrity, work ethic, trust, ability to listen well, kindness, ability to receive constructive criticism, self-accountability, and fairness.

- **Competence** is the knowledge, skills, and capabilities that we leverage in our day-to-day work. It is the technical expertise one has in whatever field one specializes in. Much of this appears on a person's bio or résumé.

Both qualities are equally important, although we haven't treated them that way in past hiring practices. We often say that leaders and organizations usually "hire for competence, and fire for character."

Underneath this brews the true passions of the individual, and the ultimate legacy they want to leave when they retire. The passions and legacy will be manifest through our character and competencies, skills, and attributes.

Lastly, this is all manifested in our public self. That is what people experience when they deal with us. That is our visible self. The words we choose, for example, will sometimes manifest our deep character traits. With the public self, both actions and words must align, or trust will decrease immediately.

Leadership Brand Creation Process

We propose eight steps that professionals can take to create a powerful leadership brand that will open doors and create opportunities.

These steps are also applicable to organizations that want to create a well-known strategic leadership brand. Simply replace the word *professional* with *organization* as you glance through this list.

The eight steps are as follows:

1. **Describe the ultimate legacy you want to leave:** Craft a one-page document, using both words and pictures, of the legacy you want to leave as a professional when you retire. Finish this one-pager by identifying why this legacy is personally important to you.

2. **Identify your greatest passion:** Take a moment to find a quiet, comfortable place where you can do this exercise. Close your eyes and calm your spirit. Then begin to paint a picture in your mind of those things that truly give you great joy. They may be activities or projects that energize you. Don't worry whether they are personal or professional at this point. Picture yourself doing each one. Open your eyes, and write down what you feel are your top three passions in life, not just work.

3. **Identify your greatest natural strengths and skills:** Brainstorm a list of natural talents you have that are very important to you. Next, categorize them into one of two different groupings: character or competence. Circle the one or two that seem to have made the biggest positive difference in your life and career.

4. **Discover patterns:** Take a moment to review your work from steps 1–3. Identify any patterns that you can make from this. What messages are these signaling to you? What fire are you feeling inside? What makes you smile? What creates confidence?

5. **Craft a unique leadership brand statement:** Now it is time to craft your own powerful leadership brand. Although you may never actually share this with others, as you compose it, pretend that you are writing it for public consumption. Be bold. Be extremely clear. To do this, try to answer in one paragraph three questions asked to you by a senior executive whom you want to associate with one

day: "what promise are you making to me as a leader if I do business with you? What is your unique value proposition to my organization and me? What do you want to be known for?"

6. **Test, validate, and refine:** Once you have an initial draft of your powerful leadership brand, take it to a few trusted others from different areas of your life who know you well, and ask them for feedback. Tell them to be honest and direct. Then use whatever feedback you received and refine your leadership brand statement.

7. **Acquire the necessary knowledge, skills, and behaviors to close gaps:** Identify what you need to do to live and breathe your new leadership brand and make it a part of your DNA. Put an improvement plan in place with milestones and accountabilities.

8. **Reintroduce yourself to important others:** Create a reintroduction game plan that identifies the most important people or organizations with which you would like to reintroduce yourself. Then identify the best way to do so using an eclectic mix of mediums: lunch dates, social media, Skype, and so forth.

You have all the power you need to reshape your leadership brand and begin to reshape the discussion around your value and possibilities.

Accelerator 4: Being a Reinvention Champion

In 2006, when Muhammad Yunus was awarded the Nobel Peace Prize, it was said that he was responsible for either directly or indirectly helping lift one billion people out of poverty. Yunus did this by inventing a new banking system called Village Banking, which used the principles of microfinance to help the poor create sustainable businesses.

From Professor to Banker of the Poor

Yunus began his career as a young professor at Chittagong College in Bangladesh. He specialized in macroeconomics and was well liked and respected by his students.

One day in 1976, he was teaching his class about his theories regarding poor people and the economics that create poverty when his mind began to drift to the poverty-stricken people just outside his classroom window. Many were lying on a neighboring lot dying of hunger. A terrible famine had gripped the entirety of Bangladesh.

When class ended, Yunus could not stop pondering the irony of how he could be teaching students about poverty at a prestigious college while people suffered tremendously just one block away. Shaken to the core, he thought, "What good are economic theories of poverty when all around me people are dying of starvation?"

Yunus decided to organize a field trip to get a better sense of poverty in local villages. He asked a few of his students to accompany him. His goal was to experience the poverty cycle firsthand. From this field trip came a deeply changed man. Yunus was ready to reinvent not only banking to the poor, but also himself as well.

THE PRINCIPLE OF ENABLING CHANGE

To enable significant change requires help from others. And those others will only willingly offer help when change facilitators walk the talk. Leaders of change espouse big, bold visions. They work both formal and informal channels to reach others to create a guiding coalition that will bust up inertia and bureaucracy.

Aligning to His True Passion

Yunus quit his job as a professor and founded Grameen Bank. This bank focused solely on giving microfinance loans to village banking councils. Yunus made sure that those he hired to help start and run the banks were people who had experienced poverty firsthand in Bangladesh.

Since those early days, Yunus and his bank have now set up thousands of village banks throughout the world. This new banking system has turned out to be so effective that there is a ninety-seven percent loan payback rate, better than any other formal banking enterprise in the world.

Today, Grameen Bank has 2,564 branches in fifty-eight countries, with 19,800 staff, and serves approximately 81,367 villages. More than eight billion dollars has been loaned to more than ten million individual borrowers since inception.

Launching Individual Reinvention

Muhammad Yunus had made a successful contribution as a professor of economics at Chittagong College. But his true passion, and his real calling in life, was diving into the economics of the poor.

For Yunus to realize his dream, he had to undergo a major professional reinvention. He transformed from being someone who "taught" about poverty to someone who actually "solved" poverty. Yunus worked hard at updating and refining his mind-set, skill set, tool set, and behavioral set in significant and revolutionary ways.

There are ten general personal attributes that Muhammad Yunus had to ensure were in place. We call these the ten Powerful Attributes of Successful Reinventors. These ten attributes are listed in the following model.

10 POWERFUL ATTRIBUTES OF
SUCCESSFUL REINVENTORS

1. Reinventors Are Dissatisfied with the Status Quo

Change will never happen without an internal felt need for change. Until the person, or leadership team, feels dissatisfaction coming from within, change will be hard to muster and sustain. Dissatisfaction with one's present situation can come because of difficult circumstances or new information that shows the current path is one of high risk.

- **Yunus Case Study:** Yunus's first sense of deep dissatisfaction came when he realized that his fellow Bangladeshi citizens were dying right outside his classroom window. That realization spurred him into his first action of visiting villages.

2. Reinventors Embrace Change

To reinvent is to change something in big ways. Reinvention must be looked upon as a glass-half-full versus glass-half-empty exercise. More than that, successful reinventors must seize upon change and focus on the benefits coming their way.

- **Yunus Case Study:** Yunus never looked back after leaving his academic duties. He pursued his new endeavor full-time and plunged headfirst into the world of village banking, social entrepreneurship, and small start-up business.

3. Reinventors Challenge Outdated and Distorted Thinking Patterns

Most huge discoveries in human history were driven because key individuals refused to accept current theories and paradigms. "The world is flat!" Columbus was told as he grew up in Europe. He felt those ideas were distorted and outdated. Because he challenged current worldviews, Columbus and his men discovered the Americas.

- **Yunus Case Study:** When Yunus first took his proposal to a local banker, his request was denied. When he asked why, the banker revealed his distorted mind-set when he said, "Poor people never pay back loans." Yunus decided to move forward with a radically different paradigm: poor people will indeed pay back their loans if they are held accountable by peers in a village banking system.

4. Reinventors Are Proactive

Proactive people "act" rather than "react." They act in accordance with the values they hold most dear. A person who must go through Reinvention, but who has the demeanor and attitude of acting only when they are forced to, will most likely find that he or she no longer has a seat on the bus. Reactive people are at the mercy of events.

- **Yunus Case Study:** Yunus not only visited the villages with his students, he also interviewed actual women in those villages who were trying to earn money to feed their families. He learned the exact amount of cash they needed to jump-start their businesses. He calculated the total amount and took it to a local bank to work win–win equations for both parties, the bank and the customer.

5. Reinventors Are Visionary

The Reinvention Formula, introduced in Chapter Three, shows that transformation requires a clear and compelling vision of a desired future state in order to energize the reinventors so they can maintain positive momentum on a daily basis. Reinventors must also take the time and effort to help others affected by the reinvention to see the future as they do.

- **Yunus Case Study:** Yunus envisioned a system of "village banking" in which bureaucracy and complex policies were shunned and replaced by locals helping locals improve their lives. Yunus had a clear picture of this alternate reality in his mind's eye, and he rallied others until they could see it, too.

(Continued)

6. Reinventors Engage Their Network

To succeed in business requires that others help you. One study showed that approximately seventy-eight percent of all jobs are filled by people whom the hiring manager knows or has been referred to. Harvard Business School recently released a report based on surveys with past graduates from their MBA program. Graduates said that even more important than their education were the relationships they forged with their classmates. Reinventors cannot do it alone.

- **Yunus Case Study:** Yunus got his initial loan by forging a partnership with a branch manager of a local bank who was willing to begin with baby steps and who trusted Yunus because of their relationship.

7. Reinventors Are Tech Savvy

So much of finding new employment or launching your own business happens through new technologies that didn't exist twenty years ago. More specifically, all reinventors need to understand social networking as a way of connecting people, opportunities, and ideas. Those individuals seeking to reinvent themselves by using the tools of the Stone Age will most likely underachieve.

- **Yunus Case Study:** Yunus applied economic principles to everything he did. He used the latest technology when opening Grameen Bank and did not shy away from leveraging new technologies to help achieve his mission of a poverty-free world.

8. Reinventors Implement Best Practices

We all have our own way of doing things. But we also know that there are some ways of doing things that produce better results than others. A best practice is simply the best way to do something. Reinventors should talk to others who have been in their situation, or search online for the best way to go about their task of reinvention.

- **Yunus Case Study:** Yunus knew that instilling borrowers with a deep sense of accountability was a best practice in terms of attaining reliable loan repayment. That is why his loan process asked that borrowers both receive and repay their loans to a small committee of people from their village. It is much harder to ignore neighbors whom they see every day than an anonymous stranger working on the twelfth floor of a big city bank.

9. Reinventors Are Resilient

The book *Raising Resilient Children* suggests that the attribute of resilience is the most important character trait that parents can teach their children. The authors argue that resilient children are able to pick themselves up after suffering difficult situations and continue and move forward with confident self-esteem. Children who aren't resilient begin to isolate themselves and go down undesirable paths. Likewise, reinventors must be resilient.

- **Yunus Case Study:** Yunus exhibited resilience when he was first turned down by the local branch manager. Instead of giving up, he returned with another proposal. Everything that the reinventor tries will not lead to success, but persistence will eventually pay off.

10. Reinventors Hold Themselves Accountable

We believe that people can't change something that they don't know about. Holding yourself accountable means measuring your performance so that you know whether or not you are progressing toward your goals. It means setting up a formal system that rewards you when you achieve your targets and disciplines you when you don't.

- **Yunus Case Study:** Notice that the primary reason Grameen Bank has an unheard-of ninety-seven-percent loan repayment rate is because the women receiving the loans are being held accountable for repayment by their peers and fellow women of the village.

The 10 Powerful Attributes of Successful Reinventors Assessment

The following worksheet helps you candidly evaluate yourself and your organization against the ten attributes spoken about.

The worksheet also contains two other rating scales that provide deep insight. The first is the "ability" rating. This rates the degree to which you are currently able to implement a particular attribute. The second is the "desire" ranking. This measures the degree to which you have sufficient desire and motivation to adopt that attribute.

To make successful change happen—and to implement the 10 attributes—it takes a powerful combination of both desire and ability.

- **Instructions:** Please complete the assessment by answering the following four questions for each reinventor attribute. Please use a scale of 1–10 (1 = poor; 5 = average; 10 = world-class).

- **Overall Score:** How well do you currently embody this attribute?

- **Ability Rating:** How strong is your ability to use this attribute effectively?

- **Desire Rating:** How strong is your desire to become better at this attribute?

- **Reasons for Scores (Root Causes):** Why might your scores be this way in regards to your mind-set, skill set, tool set, and behavioral set?

Reinventor Attribute	Overall Score	Ability Rating	Desire Rating	Reasons for Score (Root Cause)
Reinventors are dissatisfied with the status quo.				
Reinventors embrace change.				
Reinventors are proactive.				
Reinventors challenge outdated-distorted thinking patterns.				
Reinventors are visionary.				
Reinventors engage their network.				
Reinventors are tech savvy.				
Reinventors implement best practices.				
Reinventors are resilient.				
Reinventors hold themselves accountable.				

Overcoming the Law of Gravity

NASA reports that seventy percent of the total fuel used in past space shuttle flights was expended in the first ninety seconds. It took that much energy and thrust to overcome the law of gravity for the space shuttle to ascend from the launch platform.

In 2000, the director of the Kennedy Space Center invited us to sit with the space shuttle families during a particular space shuttle launch. We were only one mile away from the launch area.

At the end of the traditional countdown, smoke and fire thrust out from underneath the rocket and across the launch platform for three seconds before it began moving upward. It took ninety seconds for the shuttle to penetrate the clouds. And within a few minutes, the spacecraft was flying at three thousand miles per hour toward its target.

Breaking Free from Inertia and the Status Quo

Individuals and organizations seeking to reinvent must fuel their own liftoff and break the law of the status quo by implementing the 10 Powerful Attributes of Successful Reinventors. These attributes give reinventors the energy and momentum needed to overcome outdated mind-sets, skill sets, tool sets, and behavioral sets.

Most of the ten attributes require inside-out change. This means that it begins with a fundamental rethinking of how we see the world, our core nature, and what we choose to do on a daily basis. Inside-out change digs deep.

Accelerator 5: Preserving Work-Life Balance

It's hard to find anyone who feels good about life when they are way out of balance. Being out of balance means that the time and energy focused on one of your key areas of responsibility in your personal and professional life is all consuming and bankrupting the others.

Going through a reinvention exercise inherently means putting yourself or your organization through a time- and energy-intensive process for multiple months. It is easy to get out of balance. And while Stephen R. Covey once said that all human beings have periods of imbalance, and that is okay, what is not okay is for the reinvention effort to end up destroying value in other important relationships and focus points in your life.

We've identified five steps that reinventors can undertake that will give them the best chance to maintain a semblance of work–life balance during reinvention.

Five Steps to Maintaining Work–Life Balance

1. Identify no more then six areas of responsibility that you must do well in.

2. Identify a twelve-month vision for those areas.

3. Identify the key goals you want to accomplish in each area while reinventing.

4. Engage in weekly planning.

5. Engage in weekly accountability.

We have mocked up an example of a work–life balance plan that hopefully will help you understand what is expected of each exercise. For our example, we wrote something that might belong to a VP of Sales of a large pharmaceutical company who is married with children and active in the community.

STEPS 1-3: AREA OF RESPONSIBILITY, VISION, AND GOALS

Area of Responsibility	Twelve-Month Vision	Goals During Reinvention
Worker	To achieve my team's annual goals and metrics	Always be there for my employees and never miss scheduled interactions with them
Reinventor	To finish a personal reinvention in preparing for potential downsizing next year	To one hundred-percent fulfill my Reinvention Roadmap
Spouse	To consistently have a date night two times per month	To schedule date nights two weeks in advance and let spouse know
Mother	To attend seventy percent of my children's sports and arts performances	To schedule each week with my children's upcoming events
Friend	To tighten relationships with my three best friends	To establish proactive relationships on Facebook and Instagram
Community Member	To fulfill my goals one hundred percent as a city council member	To ask others well in advance to backfill for me if necessary

Step 4: Weekly Planning

We suggest implementing a weekly planning strategy. To do this, simply pick a thirty-minute timeslot when you can do weekly planning. Make sure it is in a quiet place where your mind can focus. Using the grid on the previous page, please do two activities during the planning period:

1. Review the six areas of responsibility and the visions you wrote about them.

2. Next, fill in the third column and write in the specific things you would like to accomplish for that area of responsibility in the coming week.

Step 5: Weekly Accountability

A best practice is to also practice personal accountability during your thirty-minute planning period. To do this, simply begin your session by reviewing how well you did in the previous week against your weekly goals. Note things that worked, and things that could have gone better.

Weekly planning around your six areas of responsibility keeps leaders focused on the larger picture rather than focused almost exclusively on one area of responsibility. We suggest that during a reinvention effort, the individual sign up for a little less in the other areas in order to be realistic regarding the time and effort reinvention takes.

Hopefully, doing weekly planning will be helpful enough that it becomes a practice that you do regardless of reinvention or not. Great things rarely happen by happenstance. They are usually blueprinted out before they are executed on.

THE PRINCIPLE OF SPEED

Customers are demanding higher standards and instant-gratification. As the world increases in spin rate, simply being fast isn't good enough. You have to be faster than anyone and everyone. Accelerate until you're number one, and then pick up the pace to stay there. Start with culture. No company in any industry or geography can accelerate with a slow culture.

Michael Jordan and the Bad Boys

Michael Jordan was at a crossroads after the 1992 NBA season. He and his Chicago Bulls teammates had just lost to the Detroit Pistons in the Eastern Conference Finals for the second season in a row. There was clearly a trend in place, and Jordan, being one of the most competitive athletes of all time in any sport, had had enough.

The Bad Boys of Detroit were not only blocking Jordan's ultimate goal of winning an NBA Championship, but they were also beating him up in the process. They employed the infamous Jordan Rules thought up by their head coach, Chuck Daly, which meant that every time Jordan drove to the basket, he usually found himself lying on his back wondering what had happened. Back in those days, the rules of the NBA were different, and most referees went by the unwritten code of "no blood, no foul."

Digging Deep

As the off-season began, Michael Jordan had a bitter taste in his mouth. He decided he would do whatever it took to break through the barrier the Detroit Pistons had put up against his Bulls. His only goal and focus that summer and coming into the 1993 season was beating the Detroit Pistons, who he knew would once again be waiting for them in the Eastern Conference Finals. That became his singular focus, and it created an incredible sense of urgency and momentum for Jordan during the off-season.

While most NBA players took the summer off, Jordan went to work.

After much soul-searching, Jordan realized that the most important thing he could do was dramatically increase his strength and bulk up.

Joe Dumars, the Piston who guarded Jordan defensively, was an extremely strong player who played Jordan really hard. And when it came to crunch time, usually games six and seven, it seemed like Dumars had a little edge. With a little more juice in the engine, Jordan felt he could probably get the Bulls over the top. So training and strength became his number-one priority over the summer.

The Breakfast Club

While most NBA players rested their bodies during the summer, Jordan established a routine of daily early-morning training in his home gym. A few other Bulls players joined in, and they began calling it the Breakfast Club.

The Breakfast Club was a daily 7:00 a.m. meet-up at his house where he and a few other players would begin their training routine. There were weight lifting and agility drills. And, at 9:00 a.m., after the workouts were over, Jordan's chef made the crew breakfast.

By the end of the summer, Jordan had added twenty-five additional pounds of muscle to his upper body, core, and legs because of the daily Breakfast Club workouts. And did he finally achieve his goal of beating the Pistons and winning an NBA Championship? Yes. In fact, by 1998 the Chicago Bulls had won a total of six championships.

Never Go It Alone

The conventional wisdom we hear throughout our lives is to never go it alone. We would submit that this is true for surrounding yourself not only with great people but also with powerful accelerators.

No reinvention, individually or organizationally, ever succeeded without the ability to move people in the pursuit of the goal. Individually, it is your ability to move yourself. Organizationally, it is your ability to move others. At their heart, all five of these accelerators are essentially about getting you and others to move in productive ways.

When one understands what it really takes to climb the tallest mountain in the world, Mount Everest, it is amazing to note the incredible amount of powerful accelerator-enablers climbers must surround themselves with to be successful. Accelerators matter.

***What powerful accelerators must you surround yourself
with to get to the top of your Everest?***

Expert Insight: Elin Hurvenes

Preparing to reinvent yourself for a new role requires a great deal of thinking about how the skills and experience you have accumulated can be relevant and put to good use in your new position. The exponential power of the five accelerators identified by the authors provides an excellent framework and boost for your own reinvention.

In my business, it is a person's executive experience that eventually helps them become an attractive nonexecutive director. But going through the five processes described in this chapter will help that person redefine their thinking and achieve crystal clarity about their contribution to boardroom discussions. If you can speak the boardroom language, your ability to impress chairmen, nomination committees, and headhunters will improve.

Key Insights

The chapter's key learning follows right along with the five reinvention accelerators:

Leader Sets

This is clearly an important accelerator for a future nonexecutive director. Fine-tuning your own mind-set to understand—and be comfortable with—the light shining on you as an executive when the going is good and being prepared to take the flack when things are tough is essential.

Whole-Brain Thinking

Use the Herrmann method to understand how you can best communicate with and influence a group of strangers. This, in essence, is what a board is when you first join.

Personal Leadership Brand

The authors suggested that "Character is at the core of who we are as individuals," and I agree. This is essential in the boardroom. You must have the courage to have an independent voice.

Being a Reinvention Champion

If you know and understand your own values and behaviors and they are aligned with the values and behaviors of the companies you represent, you can be a proactive reinventor.

Preserving Work–Life Balance

To most career women I know, preserving work–life balance is a challenge. This book provides a structure to this challenge but, above all, highlights that two brains are always better than one. It is vital that you surround yourself with good mentors, discussion partners, and sounding boards.

Application to My Career

On 22 February 2002, the population of Norway woke up to a national disruption on a grand scale. The Secretary of State for Trade and Industry, Mr. Ansgar

Gabrielsen, announced he would increase the female nonexecutive representation on boards of listed companies from six to forty percent by introducing a legal gender quota.

The legislation was fierce; it gave the government the right to delist companies from the Oslo Stock Exchange or simply close down noncompliers. It was the largest redistribution of power since women received the right to vote.

The fact is that seventy-four percent of women in Norway work compared with the Organisation for Economic Co-operation and Development average of fifty-seven percent (2014 figures). Women's entry into the labour market in the 1960s and '70s had more impact on the Norwegian national economy than striking oil in the North Sea.

Mr. Ansgar—in his courageous announcement—questioned why the talent, experience, and perspectives of the female population should not be represented at the tables of power and influence. In short, he was trying to change the mind-set of a nation.

Norwegian chairmen, nomination committees, and investors were forced to readdress their values and reasons for all-male board appointments. Were the driving forces tradition, control, and convenience, or had they genuinely always looked for the best candidates—despite systematically ignoring half the population? Mr. Ansgar, with his unprecedented method, not only changed the mind-set of a nation but also put the topic of women on boards on the global agenda.

In Europe, serving as a nonexecutive director is now a real career option for women. Each year, I have hundreds of discussions with women executives from all over the world on how they can best position themselves for these roles. The question I always ask is "How will you be able to contribute in a boardroom?" I want them to be able to articulate in their own words how they will add value. It is a practice run.

Advice to the Reader

The process of changing one's mind-set is hard. And when it is involuntary, it can also hurt. Going though the reinvention process will help you understand how your own experience can add value to your new role as an executive.

Your role is to challenge the status quo, whilst also being supportive as a team member. This can be a delicate balancing act. Disrupting executive team dynamics (or boardroom dynamics) can sometimes be necessary. But being too disruptive can be unhelpful in an environment where consensus is the ultimate goal. Reflecting on your character and behaviours by identifying your blind spots and accepting that you "don't know what you don't know" will make you more attractive and strengthen your position.

About the Expert

Elin Hurvenes is Founder and Chair of the Professional Boards Forum. She created the PBF in 2002 in response to the Norwegian government's introduction of a controversial quota law to bring 40 percent of women onto company boards. She hosted a series of innovative events for women executives, aligning them directly with company chairmen, which immediately resulted in new board appointments. Today, PBF operates in the United Kingdom, The Netherlands, Germany, Switzerland, and Norway (www.boardsforum.co.uk).

Hurvenes is also a partner at Chairman Mentors International and received her MBA at the London Business School.

Chapter Seven

◇◇◇◇◇◇◇◇◇◇◇◇◇◇◇◇◇◇◇◇◇◇◇◇◇◇◇◇◇◇◇◇◇◇

READY, AIM, REINVENT!

EXHIBITING EXCEPTIONAL LEADERSHIP IN PURSUIT OF A BETTER ENDGAME

"What lies behind us, and what lies before us,
are small matters compared to what lies within us."

—*Ralph Waldo Emerson*

Congratulations! If you've made it this far, it most likely means you're strongly considering launching a reinvention effort for either yourself or your organization.

While writing this final chapter, we asked ourselves, "What are a few send-off thoughts we might provide these courageous people?" The following is what came to mind.

A Teenage Change Agent in Pakistan

On the afternoon of October 9, 2012, a fourteen-year-old boarded her school bus in the Pakistani district of Swat. A masked gunman also boarded the bus. He shouted, "Which one of you is Malala? Speak up, otherwise I will shoot you all!" When Malala courageously identified herself, he shot her three times with his pistol. One of the bullets entered her head, crossed through her neck, and lodged into her chest.

Malala was unconscious and in critical condition for weeks. She later improved enough to begin intensive rehabilitation in Europe. When the Taliban heard that Malala had survived the assassination attempt, they reiterated their intent to kill her once and for all. And they added that her father would share the same fate.

Why would the Taliban attempt to assassinate a fourteen-year-old girl?

Two years before, the Taliban had issued an edict proclaiming that girls could not attend school in Pakistan. The terrorist group then began to destroy more than 100 girls' schools in the same region where Malala lived.

Malala, however, was determined to silence the Taliban on the issue of schooling. At the young age of twelve, she began to launch a public campaign demanding that girls be allowed to get an education.

Her father enthusiastically supported her behind the scenes.

Malala began writing a public blog for the BBC detailing her life under Taliban rule and her views on promoting education for girls. She was even bold enough to speak at public events. At one televised meeting, she exclaimed, "How dare the Taliban take away my basic right to education!"

Taking Issues into Her Own Hands

Since her recovery, Malala has launched the Special Envoy for Global Education complete with the slogan, "I am Malala." She demanded that all children worldwide, boy or girl, be in school by the end of 2015. *Time* magazine featured her on its front cover as one of "The 100 Most Influential People in the World." And she recently won the most impressive prize of all—the Nobel Peace Prize.

On Malala's 16th birthday, she spoke to the United Nations and called for worldwide access to education for all people. In her speech, she fearlessly attacked groups like the Taliban, saying,

"The terrorists thought they would change my aims and stop my ambitions, but nothing changed in my life except this:

weakness, fear, and hopelessness died. Strength, power, and courage was born . . . I am not against anyone, neither am I here to speak in terms of personal revenge against the Taliban or any other terrorist group. I'm here to speak up for the right of education for every child.

"I want education for the sons and daughters of the Taliban and all terrorists and extremists. This is not my day today, but the day of every woman, every boy, and every girl who have raised their voice for their rights."

Malala exhibited exceptional leadership in the pursuit of a better endgame. She simply stepped up and led. Leaders lead, and Malala's leadership has caused the Taliban to uncharacteristically back down on their rhetoric to kill her because of her superior leadership and her courage to stand up to bullies.

Superior self-leadership and organizational leadership are absolutely needed when launching into individual or organizational reinvention. Leadership truly is the force multiplier ultimately behind outcomes—both good and bad—at the individual, team, organizational, and societal levels.

Resiliency Matters . . . a Lot!

We spoke about the importance of resilience in an earlier chapter, but we would like to expand a bit more on this crucial skill and attribute.

Resilience, or the ability to bounce back after failure, is a key attribute of successful reinventors. Being resilient is the ability to overcome speed bumps or colossal setbacks. This is true for both individuals and organizations.

Resiliency can be seen in action through the experiences of the following five leaders.

- **J. K. Rowling:** The author of the Harry Potter series didn't magically become wealthier than the Queen of England.

Impoverished and divorced, she wrote the first book on an old typewriter. It met complete rejection by more than ten publishers. A year later, Barry Cunningham agreed to publish her book, but suggested she get another job because children's books typically produced meager profits. Rowling has just become a billionaire.

- **Steve Jobs:** Although your iPhone, Mac, or iPad seem indispensable today, two decades ago you probably would have dismissed Apple products altogether. Jobs's Apple III computer, the early model of the Mac, was so poorly designed that the computer earned a reputation as an unreliable machine that invariably crashed. After Jobs was fired from Apple, he designed the NeXT hardware, which sold poorly at first but later became the foundation for future Apple products. He also created Pixar. And the rest is history.

- **Thomas Edison:** The inventor of the light bulb, phonograph, and motion picture camera once said, "If I find 10,000 ways something won't work, I haven't failed. I am not discouraged, because every wrong attempt discarded is another step forward." Imagine if Edison gave up after the 9,999th time!

- **Walt Disney:** The man who gave us Disneyland navigated a very rocky road before becoming a legend. His first cartoon series in Kansas City left him bankrupt. An editor fired Disney because he believed he was unimaginative. Disney even lost rights to his first commercially successful character, Oswald the Lucky Rabbit. Then Mickey Mouse and Donald Duck happened, and it was time to create Disney magic.

- **Albert Einstein:** Although we use the name Einstein to dub someone a genius, the scientist's teachers believed that he was mentally challenged. In fact, he was unable to speak fluently until age twelve. He was expelled from high school at age sixteen for failing several subjects. It wasn't until he reached the age of eighteen that he pursued his interest in calculus and physics. He used his unconventional mind to formulate the groundbreaking theory of relativity and change the face of modern physics.

In order to claim eventual fame, these people were faced with obstacles that required them to embrace their mistakes and continue forward with steadfast determination. Sometimes failure, or even many failures, precedes success.

Malala Yousafzai might be the most resilient of all. The following quote sums up her internal fortitude to carry on with resilience no matter the difficulties in her path:

I don't want to be remembered as the girl who got shot. I want to be remembered as the girl who stood up.

It seems that, in the 21st-century business jungle, only the resilient survive.

Focus on the "D"

Elon Musk, the South African entrepreneur who is now being compared to Henry Ford for his revolutionary work with Tesla Autos, saw a large chink in the automobile industry's armor because of their inability to begin innovating toward the gasless automobile of the future. He clearly saw an industry ripe for destruction.

This was the industry, after all, that tried to trick the public in the 1980s by simply adding a few shiny features to a Chevrolet, putting a Cadillac nameplate on it, and hoping to pass it off as a luxury car.

Today, Tesla is well ahead of the competition in terms of using alternative energy sources and innovative features throughout the car. And there is no lack of buyers as every Tesla is gobbled up. The lesson here is that both auto customers and disruptive auto entrepreneurs were hugely dissatisfied with the car industry and teamed up to disrupt the Big Three. Detroit seems to operate without dissatisfaction with the status quo and remarkably continues to do just enough to get by.

Without strong dissatisfaction, antibiotics are never discovered, the printing press arrives a century later, Rocky doesn't knock out Apollo Creed, and Cinderella skips the ball. Without the "D," significant change will not happen. This is why the "D" is the first element in the Reinvention Formula.

What can you do when you know that Reinvention is the best remedy, but that the "D" is just not where it needs to be? We have found two strategies that tend to work well.

First, doing a benchmark exercise in which you scan the level of performance of similar companies is powerful. Second, conducting a general scan of your external environment—customers, stakeholders, and industry trends—seems to create better awareness and new insights that create conviction for change.

When Ripples Disrupt

It isn't just massive shockwaves that disrupt your world. Shockwaves often spin off disruptive ripples that are less awe-inspiring than shockwaves, but are disruptive nonetheless. These ripples often hit certain industries and create unmistakable undulations in the business environment.

Consider a strong ripple that is currently passing through the restaurant industry. What is the disruption? Mobile food trucks. Walk around any downtown area during the workday, and you'll see them everywhere—along with the lines of customers waiting for service.

Kogi BBQ has been drawing crowds since 1998, when two friends decided to create a fusion between Korean BBQ and Mexican tacos and then hawk them from the streets of Los Angeles. Food trucks weren't new to the streets of Los Angeles, but this type was.

For years, old trucks known as "roach coaches" lined construction sites offering cheap eats. But no one had ever brought restaurant-quality gourmet food to the streets before. Kogi's owners began using social media to alert urbanites as to where they would be stopping throughout the day.

Scott Steinberg, a business strategist, suggests that we can all learn simple lessons about disruptive change and reinventive companies from the success of gourmet mobile food trucks.

- **Emphasize your assets and strengths:** Food trucks had a bad reputation until a few crafty chefs unlocked the potential of "food on wheels" by taking advantage of the naturally low overhead, mobility, and gourmet cooking.

- **Spread the word:** Food trucks have been experts at tapping into social media and networking to build buzz within local businesses and the employees who staff them. They often have a cult following.

- **Be bold and flexible:** With so little at stake, mobile food truck owners feel free to experiment and try new things. If something isn't working, scrap it and try something new.

- **Say no to negativity:** Be innovative—see opportunities where others see roadblocks. And don't concentrate on what you don't have, but what you do have.

We don't know of any industry that hasn't been impacted by at least a few of the 20 global shockwaves. We are even more confident that rampant rippling is taking place in every nook and cranny of the world.

Coming Soon: A New Type of Global Shockwave

Each year the World Economic Forum releases their annual Global Risks Report. It has the input of more than nine hundred of the world's leading experts to determine the perceived impact and likelihood of twenty prevalent global risks over the next ten years.

THE TOP 10 MOST LIKELY GLOBAL RISKS

- Interstate Conflict
- Extreme Weather
- Failed Governments
- State Collapse
- Unemployment
- Natural Catastrophes
- Climate Change
- Water Crises
- Data Theft
- Cyber Attacks

The 2015 report boldly stated that the most pressing threat to the stability of the world in the next decade would be international conflict. The direct impact of those conflicts will create a severe water crisis across the planet. The report ends by concluding that environmental risks will be far graver than economic ones as we head further into the 21st century. The Age of Disruption indeed.

In Chapter 1, we described the Age of Disruption in detail and identified twenty global shockwaves that have occurred since 1981 that seem to be the root behind our current environment.

Our research shows that there have been five different types of global shockwaves that have challenged the world's status quo: economic, technology, global competition, management theory, and geo-political. Going forward it seems likely that another new category of global shockwave will roll inland: an environmental-climate shockwave.

Sharpening Your Reinvention Saw

The story is told of two sawing teams having a competition in the woods. The two-man teams were using a two-person saw and were focused completely on the thick log in front of them. Both teams felt pressure to win as their peers were watching their contest with great delight.

Midway through the competition, one of the teams suddenly stopped sawing. They good-naturedly sat down, pulled out a saw sharpener, and began sharpening their saw.

The other team could not believe what they were seeing. What were these guys doing? The crowd even began taunting the team sharpening their saw.

The team still sawing began to saw even faster, hoping to quickly end the competition. But an interesting thing happened. As hard as they were sawing, they were making little progress.

Meanwhile, the other team finished sharpening their saw, once again took up their positions, and went to work. Because their saw was now incredibly sharp, they made quick work of the log and won the competition.

Each of us would benefit as professionals if we consistently scheduled time during the workweek to sharpen our saw, or our organization's saw. Based upon what you learned in Chapter Three, we would call this Degree 1 change, or continuous improvement. It might require staying on the lookout for new things to learn and new ways of thinking about the same old thing. Maybe it is giving your leadership team industry trade magazines and having them report out in staff meetings any new market or industry changes.

More importantly, however, sharpening your reinvention saw keeps you in reinvention shape and ensures you are much more prepared to act quickly and reinvent when the need arises.

You Are Ready to Launch!

Let's return to the idea of Leader Sets.

As we mentioned, the four components of Leader Sets are crucial for change to actually stick and take hold. Leader Sets truly are how your wishes are made to happen.

We hope that you have had a positive mind-set shift while reading this book. Hopefully you were able to learn several skill sets and tool sets that will help you when reinventing. Now it is up to you to make it all happen by implementing new behavioral sets. As the wise Peter Drucker once said, "All grand strategies eventually degenerate into work."

We will leave you with one more closing chapter thought, this one by Edward Abbey:

May your trails be crooked, winding, lonesome, dangerous, but leading to the most amazing views.

ACKNOWLEDGMENTS

Shane

- **Professors:** For making my MBA experience memorable and for continuing to add value to my life well beyond my formal schooling. Specifically, to Lee Perry, John Bingham, Warner Woodworth, John Norton, Gibb Dyer, and Alan Wilkins.

- **Colleagues:** For pushing my thinking to a higher level of effectiveness. Specifically, to Bill Adams, Norm Smallwood, Rajesh Setty, Mark Oborn, Stephen M. R. Covey, Mark Rhodes, Ann Herrmann, Starr Eckholdt, Ron Axtell, Bill Snyder, Tyler England, Mark Richards, Pat McLagan, Sumukh Setty, Lisa Wardle, and Tim Clark.

- **Clients:** For allowing me to perform surgery on their organizations and being incredible partners in the process of forming solutions that made a difference. Specifically, to Hall Looney (Shea Homes), Dr. Phillip Meade (NASA), Captain Stephanie Johnson (US Navy), Sean Hoffman (KPMG), Bill Inglis (Meritage Homes), John Mayes (Yale University), Paul Madsen (Merck), Elliot Ng (Air National Guard), Mark Bowen (Mobil Oil), Jeff Clark (JD Clark), Chris Harrison (Camelot Homes), Rob Anderson (Equitable Life and Casualty), Cameron Martin (Utah Valley University), and John Houston and Sam Quigley (Intermountain Electronics).

Kate

- **Professors:** What can I say about Dr. Linda Hill? She took me under her wing while at Harvard Business School and gave me someone to model my thinking after. Despite her extreme obligations as chief leadership guru at HBS, Linda has been an amazing support to me, always willing to lend a helping hand and meeting me as a coach. And my other teachers, all of whose collective insights inform these pages.

- **Colleagues:** I have been blessed with so many extraordinary colleagues that many of their thumbprints are on these pages: Rob Galford (my personal first responder in a professional crisis); Jean Williams (unfailing in providing intelligent feedback on anything I shot her way); Paige Hinkson (for pushing on the practical); Dina Proctor (for bringing in the spiritual); Ravi Gundlapalli (whose ability to create metaphors is unparalleled); Judy Robinette (whose enthusiastic support spurred me on to greater heights); Michelle Del Rosario (whose dry pragmatism keeps me honest); Mike "Colonel" Harper (who drove me nuts but taught me lots); and Martha Putnam Sites, Colleen Shean and Walter Carleton, Karen Shepherdson, Adel Jayasuria, Lily Wong, Sabri Rawi, Ripa Rashid, Michael Kossler, Rajeev Peshawaria (Malaysia, boleh!). And last, but by no means least, Dr. Redha Bebehani who is always willing to engage with us and bring our ideas to market.

- **Clients:** If the toughest clients are the greatest teachers, then I must start with my friends at Verizon, notably Denis Sullivan and Jeff Kudlata. It was your high standards that enabled all of us to gain the global recognition that came our way. If the kindest clients are always good for a pick-me-up, then that distinction goes to Robert Burnside of Ketchum. This is a knowledgeable gentleman if I ever saw one, and he was a partner-in-crime with Barri Rafferty and Rob Flaherty. And to Ian Gee (Nokia); Phil Lichtenfels (Bristol-Myers Squibb); Phil Birkin and Beth Cliff (EMC); Cary Friedman (Goldman Sachs and Credit Suisse); Steffen Landauer (Goldman Sachs); Valerie Yanni (Endurance Insurance); Emily Dancygere King (Citigroup); and Judy Rabinowitz (BNP Paribas). Also, a big thanks to Maybank, AmBank, Telekom Malaysia, and Indian Railways for helping me to see the universality of leadership principles around the globe.

SweetmanCragun

- **Partners:** The following have supported our new firm as we try to make our own little dent in the universe. Specifically, to Rajesh Setty, David Covey, Stephan Mardyks, Kevin Wheeler, Ravi Gundlapalli, and Jason Franzen.

- **Editors:** This book could not have been at the level it is without the terrific help of Judith Ross, our editor, who delivers incisive editorial critiques with such grace and good humor that we leap to respond. She is our steel magnolia. Thanks to Kelly Messier, whose keen eye for detail will not allow even the most slender comma to fall through the cracks.

- **Publisher:** For the wonderful folks at Greenleaf Book Group for truly engaging us in a win–win partnership. Specifically, to Justin Branch.

- **Book Reviewers:** Thanks to the following book reviewers: Mark Heslop, Dustin Cragun, Davis Cragun, Chase Cragun, Dave Ulrich, Norm Smallwood, Rob Galford, Stephan Mardyks, David Covey, Phillip Meade, and Linda Hill.

AUTHOR Q&A

Q: Completing your first book together must feel satisfying. Can you discuss some of the joys and challenges of this experience?

A: This is the first time we've written a book together, and it has been a gratifying experience to say the least. Our styles are complementary, as are our overall skill sets. When we initially came together, we made a quick decision to swing for the fence—to make our own little dent in the universe by being bold and writing to, and serving, a global audience. We took our three favorite authors—Covey, Collins, and Gladwell—and tried to impart a little of their style in our writing: principles, metaphors, and eclectic examples.

Q: What made you choose the importance of reinvention for this book?

A: The topic seemed to pick us for two reasons. First, we have extensive experience in individual and organizational change. And second, it seems the overwhelming concern right now with global leaders is, "Does my company have leaders that can lead in this tumultuous 21st century?" Being a master change agent and having the ability to pivot rapidly, proactively, and in quantum ways is becoming a competency that leaders today and tomorrow must master.

Q: What makes your book different from other books on the same topic?

A: There are a lot of great books on the subject of individual and organizational change. In fact, our colleagues have written some of these. It seems new ideas build on the ideas of others. We do think, however, that our book is the only business book that prescribes a powerful yet basic formula for quantum and rapid change that works equally well for both individuals and organizations. The notion that 21st-century competitiveness will be based largely upon the degree to which internal change exceeds the rate of external change seems to be something that hasn't been fully articulated on a large scale. We believe that our book is the first to identify the fundamental global shockwaves that have created the business environment we all work in—the Age of Disruption.

Q: In your work as business consultants, you see clients with a range of needs and challenges—in the United States and around the world. What is something you feel a book can do to help clients, and when do you believe those clients would be better served by working directly with you?

A: Our sense is that well-written books with new and groundbreaking perspectives help shift paradigms—the worldviews of people reading them. These types of books provide answers for the problems being faced by individuals and organizations. In terms of working with clients, one of us spent a significant portion of our career at FranklinCovey. Stephen R. Covey used to talk about "the knowing-doing gap." When we help clients implement the material in our books, we help close that gap. We help clients translate our ideas into actual behaviors. Often this results in a systemic approach; clients not only acquire new skills and knowledge, but they experience more aligned processes, systems, and structures along with more directionally correct strategies.

Q: Speaking of international clients, can you speak to the differences you've seen in businesses around the globe?

A: The only differences between geographical regions of the world and their need for reinvention are scale, scope, and points of emphasis. We are learning that *all* parts of the globe need the competency to sense incoming global shockwaves, and then to reinvent themselves in a way that accelerates remarkable results and a sustainable competitive advantage. We were recently in Egypt and Kuwait with a banking client. Before we arrived, we wondered to what degree our reinvention material would be relevant to the Middle East, and particularly in Kuwait, where government intervention is strong. To our surprise, the leaders in these countries deeply embraced the idea of reinvention, and were using the metaphors and models immediately, proclaiming, "This is exactly what we need!"

Q: Many people owe their career successes to moments of serendipity, or being in the right place at the right time. Others credit their determination. How have you two arrived at this point in your careers?

A: Three things: hard work, mentors, and relationships. We cannot overstress the importance of mentors in their ability to teach you the tools of the trade and guide you throughout the winding path of your career. And, of course, in the management consulting and training space it is all about relationships of trust and assisting one another.

Q: The tone of your book is one of urgency: if companies don't get busy with reinvention, if they don't work on being flexible and adaptable, they may find themselves trailing in the dust. If you'd written this book five years ago, what might you have said the most important trait was? What has changed between then and now?

A: The need to be flexible, adaptable, humble, and actively engaged in changing the organization has been firmly in place since the Age of Disruption was launched in the early 1980s. The difference now is the degree, intensity, and scale to which these attributes need to be modeled. As we noted in our introductory chapter, it seems the key word in the '80s was "CHANGE." Organizations needed to be able to adapt and change to meet global competitive threats. Then in the '90s, thanks to Hammer's book *Reengineering the Corporation*, the key word seemed to be "REENGINEER"— completely rethinking business and manufacturing processes. The 2000–2010 decade seemed to push the notion of change even further by stressing the need to "TRANSFORM" your organi- zation—to rethink every piece of the enterprise. We're suggest- ing that the key word in the 21st century will be "REINVENT," or the need to not only rethink every piece of the organization, but to do so in rapid, quantum, and proactive ways. We remem- ber our client projects in the 1990s and early 2000s being six- to twelve-month endeavors. Today, you wouldn't even be in the discussion if you stuck to those timeframes; instead, consultants must be able to facilitate major change for their clients within three to four months.

Q: Many business books focus on success stories; but your book includes a handful of company failures. Do you think business leaders can learn more from one or the other—failures or suc- cesses? Why did you include failures in this book?

A: We have found that when you look at both success and failure examples side-by-side, a complete picture seems to appear. The "what not to do" seems to translate straight across to the "what must we do." It validates your initial hypothesis in powerful ways. One interesting thing about our proposed methodologies, models, and principles is that they are industry and geographically agnostic. We feel they are true principles of individual and organizational change that apply in any circumstance.

Q: What is some of the most surprising insight you've gained over the years as you've worked with clients?

A: In almost every case, leaders and employees generally want to do the right thing when they come to work. They want to make a difference. But a company's strategy, culture, processes, systems, and structures play tremendous roles in what kind of behaviors, attitudes, and feelings you get from leaders and employees. The whole idea that organizations are perfectly designed to get the results that they get might be the most powerful organizational principle there is. Organizations truly get what they design for; if you want different results, you've got to change your design of strategies, culture, processes, systems, and structures—as we discuss in the book.

Q: What do you think the "Insights" from experts add to your book?

A: So many business books stay in the US-centric perspective. This means our international friends have to try to translate the message to their unique culture. Our big thought was this: why write chapter summaries and regurgitate our own medicine? Why not have experts from different regions of the world, from different industries, in different roles, shed light on our reinvention principles and give a global perspective after each chapter? We think readers will not only learn from this, but they will get the message that we truly tried to write a global business book.

Q: It's often said that business values trickle down from the top—that beliefs and values held among those in the C-suite will influence the company's entire culture. Have you ever seen this not hold true? Have you, for example, seen an instance in which a CEO has been open to change, while others in the company have resisted?

A: We have always said that unless the vast majority within an organization is feeling strong dissatisfaction with the current state, don't even bother to launch a reinvention effort. CEOs and executive teams can initiate a change effort, but they cannot control the day-to-day actions of front line employees, even if those employees have agreed to make changes. We believe they are only going to sign up for a new way of doing things if: 1) they have a strong dissatisfaction with the current state; and 2) they are clear about what's in it for them. We do, however, have strategies that we often suggest to executive teams that will help create a sufficient feeling of dissatisfaction within the employee base so that a reinvention effort can proceed.

Q: Is there a question you wish companies would ask you—one that is less obvious but will yield greater results?

A: Many leaders still believe "restructuring" is the answer to their performance problems. They think simply moving people around into different boxes, changing reporting relationships, and eliminating positions will make huge differences in results. That is tantamount to moving the deck chairs around on the *Titanic*. As we mentioned before, the idea that organizations are perfectly designed to get the results that they get suggests that it is about "systemic change" and not just about changing one component, such as structure. It is about making choices in strategies, processes, systems, structure, and culture—and tightly aligning them—to get difference results. We would like to see this idea take hold among leaders, rather than seeing them rely on quick structural fixes to make quarterly earnings.

Q: There are a lot of management consultants out there with unique ways of perceiving and solving problems. What defines your style?

A: We try to stick with espousing principles that seem to be universal and unchanging, along with our viewpoint that everything must be approached systemically. And when we do client engagements, we know that the solutions must come, and must be owned, by the client; and that it is simply our role to help them discover the right things to do.

Q: Is there anything you didn't have space to explore in this book?

A: We would have liked to have provided a lot more detail on the eleven exercises someone goes through for reinvention, but recognize that would have turned the book into more of an academic field guide. So those exercises are now on our www .ageofdisruption.com website. We also would have liked to talk more about our vision of leadership as it pertains to Leader-Accelerators, but we will take that up in our next book.

Q: Finally, if you could name the single most significant concept or piece of information you hope your readers will take away after reading *Reinvention*, what would it be and why?

A: Probably that it's better to change *before* you have to than *because* you have to, and it's important to use a formula that creates designed change rather than random change.

ABOUT SWEETMANCRAGUN

◇◇◇◇◇◇◇◇◇◇◇◇◇◇◇◇◇◇◇◇◇◇◇◇◇◇◇◇◇◇◇◇◇◇◇◇

SweetmanCragun enables clients to significantly increase the number of Leader-Accelerators at every position within the organization. Clients also convert Leader-Decelerators into Leader-Accelerators. This is critical as Leader-Decelerators suck the life out of people and processes. Everyone, and everything, is suboptimized and eventually grinds to a halt.

SweetmanCragun delivers primary services, such as consulting, training, coaching, mentoring, publishing, and mobile apps in disruptive ways that today's digital crowd eagerly devours.